A Puppy Called Aero

A Puppy Called Aero

How a Labrador Saved a Boy with ADHD

LIAM CREED
with
JOSHUA BURT

JOHN MURRAY

First published in Great Britain in 2009 by John Murray (Publishers)
An Hachette UK Company

I

A CIP catalogue record for this title is available from the British Library

Hardback ISBN 978-1-84854-048-4
Trade paperback ISBN 978-1-84854-144-3

Typeset in 11.5/14 Monotype Bembo by Servis Filmsetting Ltd, Stockport, Cheshire

Printed and bound by Clays Ltd, St Ives plc

John Murray policy is to use papers that are natural, renewable and recyclable products and made from wood grown in sustainable forests. The logging and manufacturing processes are expected to conform to the environmental regulations of the country of origin.

John Murray (Publishers)
338 Euston Road
London NW1 3BH

www.johnmurray.co.uk

To all those who had faith in me.

Contents

Prologue

Hello there. Is that a good way to start? I think it probably is. I haven't written a book before, so I'm not really familiar with the right ways to kick things off. So 'hello' it is. My name is Liam Creed, and by the time you read this I'm probably seventeen or eighteen years old. I'm tall, very tall indeed, in fact: about six foot three or four. I have longish hair, I'm quite thin, and my girlfriend used to describe my face as 'angular', whatever that means. I'm convinced that it means I'm very handsome, although after years of scowling around changing winds, my face can look a little aggressive at times. Even when I don't want it to.

Until a couple of years ago, I was trouble. I have Attention Deficit Hyperactivity Disorder (ADHD), and it was causing all kinds of problems at school. I was close to getting thrown out for good. The teachers had become understandably sick and tired of my behaviour, and they were running out of ideas as to what on earth to do with me. Detention didn't really work; in fact, I had it pencilled into my diary most weeks, and I wasn't overly fussed about getting excluded. If I'm being honest – which I guess I have to be – school didn't want me, and I didn't particularly want school either.

I'm from Chichester, born and raised. I live at home with my mum, dad, brother (Mathew) and sister (Sophie). Growing up in a small town in rural Sussex, where everything runs a hundred miles slower than a snail's pace, can be a bit of a problem when you've got a disorder with the word 'hyperactivity' in it. You tend to stand out, because everyone else seems to be so calm and at peace with their gorgeous surroundings.

So life might be nice and peaceful here for some, but for me it has only ever made the chaos in my head seem even louder. Chichester is one of those attractive, quiet cathedral towns that lots of people no doubt want to retire to some day. Basically, it's absolutely fantastic for adults, but more like hell if you're a teenager. Especially a 'troubled' one.

Most people here just want to live an easy life, to go to work, walk the dog, have a nice meal on a Friday night, do some gardening or go for a walk in the countryside over the weekend. My mum's a bit like that, and who could blame her? After a day at work she's knackered, and wants to spend some quality time on the comfiest sofa, and relax.

Unfortunately, it hasn't quite worked out that way. The main problem is me. I've spent most of my life making sure – albeit not always on purpose – that people don't relax when I'm around.

My usual routine as a teen was to stomp home, have an argument with someone on the way, or with Mum once I got there, go to my room in a huff and watch the telly, or play games on the computer, or destroy something. At the weekends I would invariably have too much time on my hands so would get up to mischief, and would end up hurting someone or destroying something, ensuring that the family could never rely on having a moment's peace.

Until, that is, a dog called Aero came into my life and changed all that. Now, I don't want you to get the wrong impression of me at the start. I know that what I've described to you so far is a troubled teen; it sounds like I'm one of those shady characters in hooded tops with knives and drugs, but I'm not one of those. I have a mental disorder that means I'm not socially as good as most people, and I can come across as surly and rude. The filter between my brain and my mouth isn't as efficient as it should be at times, and I find myself saying things that I probably shouldn't say, and I swear far too much – although I'm trying to cut down on the language.

You'll be pleased to know that any trace of abhorrent gutter talk has been edited out of this book. That was mainly my idea, so feel free to assume descriptive swear-words, but don't expect to read them.

Thankfully I'm not at school any more; that particular trauma has come to an end, and voluntarily I might add. I wasn't kicked out. I managed a few GCSEs, and I now go to college, studying construction and joinery. That's plan B, in case my dreams don't work out as planned. Once a week, I head out into the countryside to look after the pups. Much more of that to come later.

Anyone with experience of ADHD will appreciate that writing this book was a long, arduous slog for me, but it was a story that needed to be told. Because while some homes can be dominated and destroyed by the presence of someone with mental health issues, my story is proof that there is hope, that life can still be rich and glorious. We can cope with our condition in the right environment. Strangely and unexpectedly, my miracle environment turned out to be a dog-training facility a few miles away from my house.

Enjoy the book.

I

Here comes trouble

I'm sure, were you to ask anyone about their first memory, it would be something quite sweet. Perhaps a day at the zoo with the family, or a brilliant birthday party, surrounded by their friends, complete with jelly, ice cream and massive shiny presents – they might even have photographic evidence to nudge the recollection. Mine isn't quite so cutesy. My first memory is of being about four years old, covered in mud, ripping up plants in the back garden at home.

Our garden isn't terribly big, but Mum and Dad have always taken great pride in it, as though it were a little sparkling trinket – it has a regal look about it a lot of the time. My memory is just a series of flashes, nothing particularly lucid, but from what I can piece together, I'd taken a fascination with a daffodil or some such, and like any tot, my reaction was to give it a podgy-fingered prod, poke, and before you knew it, I was yanking the plant from the soil like a giant maniac uprooting a tree. I gleefully continued with my splurge of vandalism until Mum caught sight of me from the kitchen window – speckled with flying mud and flowers everywhere. She now chuckles in hindsight because I was wearing a T-shirt with Mr Messy emblazoned across the front, so they'd kind of asked for it. I have small patches of memory of her crying, and I'm not sure whether it's my over-imaginative side getting a little bit carried away, but I'm fairly sure those daffs went into the big metal bin, making for a strangely beautiful image. Even then I was secretly artistic.

I'd love to say that daffodil-gate was a one-off, but it was far from it: my irrational acts of destruction became a feature throughout my childhood. Even now, I can feel myself veering towards vandalism when I'm especially frustrated. It's a strange urge, I expect, but it feels quite normal to me. I've spent hours and hours, probably stretching into days, talking to various doctors and therapists about my destructive side. My theory, helped by some of these sessions, is that the random acts of violence towards inanimate objects were my way of taking revenge on the world. After all, if my world wasn't going to accept me as I was, I wasn't going to do the same back. Does that make sense? It has a strange logic about it, I think.

I've been asked a million times what it's like to have ADHD, and of course, to me, it's just normal, part of my everyday life. It would be easy for me to blame all my bad behaviour on being ill, but I try not to use it as an excuse – like any kid, when I'm being bad, I know I'm being bad. The point about ADHD is that things tend to happen before you've had much of a chance to make an educated decision on what you're doing, so in the case of the daffodils in the garden, my urge to tear them from the ground was far greater than my desire to keep Mum and Dad happy. Or at least, the urge came before the chance to consider what I was doing. That's the problem with ADHD; as I've got older and more inclined to recognize when I'm having a bit of a funny turn, I can almost hear my voice in the background shouting at myself to calm down and take a breath, but a lot of the time it's too late. I will already be in the middle of the hurricane. The trouble I got into changed over the early years; it started with domestic vandalism, then once I was introduced to other kids my age, they too became victims of my outbursts.

Prior to what turned out to be a monumental turnaround in my life (much, much more of that later), I generally got home from school in a bad mood, sometimes having had an argument with someone en route, had an argument with Mum about something inconsequential, went to my room and played computer games, or watched the telly if there was anything good on Sky. The only light relief was sneaking outside for a cigarette and scowling into the night, my mind hopping from one topic to another at breakneck speed.

By the weekend, all that pent-up energy would have nowhere else to go other than in the direction of trouble. On Saturday night I might go to the cinema in town if there was a good film showing, but more often than not I'd find myself traipsing round the town centre, listening to music, and trying to find ways to entertain myself. This inevitably ended in a trail of destruction. I was never about to mug an old lady or anything, or whizz off in a stolen car. Generally I'd just lollop around kicking a stone, trying to look hard, getting into mischief.

According to Mum I was rude, had an attitude problem and wouldn't do as I was told. Sounds like your average teenager to me, but I suppose it can get pretty annoying having a wise-cracking kid who's so awkward around himself that he can't get along with anyone else. Okay, so I'm playing it down – I was hell on wheels. But how did all this start?

Mum said she knew I was different right from the get-go. She hoped I was just a naughty baby, and struggled between trying not to blame me and trying not to blame herself. I already had a brother, Mathew, who was sixteen months older than me. She hadn't had a problem with him, so she knew something wasn't quite right with me. But up until I was four – around the time of the pretty daffodils – it wasn't that bad. After all, how much trouble can a round and pink baby that can only crawl and wear nappies get into? Okay, so I cried a lot, but other than my tetchy nature it was all pretty regular stuff, so Mum couldn't put her finger on what was different about me.

But when I hit four I turned into a tearaway tot.

I screamed like a dummy-wielding maniac if I didn't get my own way. Sharing toys was a war zone, and I was like a real-life Action Man making sure that no one invaded my territory. My biggest problem was interacting with the other tots. I just didn't get them. From the start I knew they were not like me. They were calmer than me. I could see them, sitting there all obedient and well behaved. Even though it's impossible to remember that time of life with any sense of clarity, I still experience an inner feeling, one that has followed me around for most of my life, that looks at other people – be they my age, older or younger – and I suspect that they are not peas from the same pod as me. They're having a whole different experience of this life thing we've got happening.

Thankfully the lady in charge of playgroup, Mrs Fuller, was friends with Mum, so she was patient and kind with me – although she was less happy when I slyly nicked a toy (namely a cuddly elephant) from the group and smuggled it home under my jumper and stained Mr Messy T-shirt.

My poor older brother Mathew bore the brunt of my toy-based tantrums; he was so cheerful and good-natured that he seemed like an angel next to me, so I'd go out of my way to make his life hell. In hindsight I was probably jealous, even then. My outbursts mainly took the form of hitting Mathew on the head with anything I could get my hands on, or screaming at him for snaffling my toy elephant. I'd stolen that for me, damn it! It must have looked so strange to see the younger brother in a family bullying his older brother – shouldn't it be the other way around? But, as with everyone, I couldn't grasp why he wasn't like me. This was my family, we had the same parents, we went on the same trips together, we wore pretty much the same clothes. And yet he was yin to my yang. I couldn't stand it. I'd steal his belongings as revenge.

In fact, talking of theft, I'd even manage to steal food from the fridge and hide it round the house. There wasn't any real reason for this – I've always been a big fan of food, and have nothing against it. I just preferred trouble, or, more likely, attention. Mum says that if she turned her back on me for a second I'd be up to some kind of mischief. But what she noticed most was that, unlike most kids, I didn't learn from my telling-offs. She could shout at me, repeat something a thousand times, and it wouldn't make any difference to me. I was like one big, toddling, mischievous brick wall. Mum says that she'd known lots of families with brats for kids, but they knew what to do when the brats became too brattish and unmanageable. With me, it seemed to be a guessing game, only one that was rigged. There didn't appear to be a correct answer.

And, sorry, but it gets even worse. You're just going to have to bear with me, I'm afraid. As with most stories with an uplifting ending, the beginning isn't quite so pretty. My childhood had spatterings of good times, lots of laughter and joy, but it wasn't an easy period. In hindsight I can see that Mum was probably often right on the edge of her nerves, and that Dad spent most of his free time away from work taking me off Mum's hands. I can now only imagine how cheerful and relieved he must have felt as the weekends came to an end, and he could get away from the madhouse and return to work. Of course, he's a big man with a massive heart and bundles of love for his family, so I don't think he'd ever admit to that even if it were the truth. All I know is that I wouldn't blame him one iota if it was. Which it isn't . . .

Anyway, yes, when my sister Sophie came along that year things got a whole lot worse.

My parents put it down to jealousy. Until then, I'd been the baby of the family, and all the attention was focused on me – even if it was often for all the wrong reasons. I could kick, scream and tantrum to my heart's content and everyone would at least still think I was cute, just because I was the youngest.

Suddenly everyone was cooing over another small bundle of pink, crying, baby blubber.

But Mum was wrong. My downward spiral wasn't because of Sophie. I *loved* babies.

Yes, let me repeat that. I, turbo-toddler from hell, loved babies.

It took a while for my mum to work it out.

It seems that I was the first person to visit the hospital to give Sophie a big cuddle. Mum must have been terrified watching me approach a dinky little baby, what with my habit of destroying pretty much everything fragile I came into contact with, but seeing me gently put my chubby arms round this tiny baby in a loving cuddle made Mum go, 'Wow.' She didn't know it back then, but every kid with ADHD has one of these wow factors. Something they're *really, really* good at despite their inability to do or say anything else right. Mine was babies, and later pets. Which explains a lot about why Aero and I get along so well. He was part of my wow factor. It just took time for everyone to work out what it was and how to hardwire into it.

All that aside, and taking everything into account, however, I was still a really horrible little kid. That's not a nice thing to say, especially about yourself. But it's true. Children have development stages, where they learn how to behave and how to interact with other people. I merrily sailed past them all, missing each one by a mile. I was on a collision course with other people, and no one could slow me down to stop it happening.

But it was a totally different story when a baby gurgled its way into the room. I'd switch from demon child to angel in a second. After I'd given my little sister a smiley welcome in the hospital (I think Mum was too knackered to notice how weird my niceness was), my fascination with Sophie continued when she arrived back home. I loved to play with her. Everything about her entertained me: her little lemon-coloured Babygro, the way her tiny fingers could clamp around my thumb with terrifying strength, the teddy bear mobile her big eyes stared at before she fell asleep. When she was a little bigger, I liked to feed her too, chortling as she slopped baby goo food down her bib. And there's more. Now this bit is hard to believe, but Mum assures me it's true – *I even changed her nappies.* Loved to, apparently. I didn't mind cleaning up a small, defenceless creature. I simply loved to look after those more appealing and less able than myself.

9

If you were my age or older, or you didn't have four legs and a smelly fur coat, I was a nasty critter, but otherwise – a perfect angel.

I think it confused Mum, but it gave her hope too.

There were times when she really was at her wits' end with me. Maybe, if she hadn't seen how I reacted to my sister, and later on how I bonded with neighbours' babies and pets, she might have written me off as a bad job. No doubt she searched for a 666 on my scalp a fair few times, worrying I'd come along straight from a starring role in a horror film. But my caring behaviour with babies and cuddly animals was like a breath of fresh air for her. Every time I kicked someone, something, anything; smashed vases; pushed expensive ornaments off tables; sat cross-legged in the garden systematically dismantling a flowerbed, she clung to the memory of my moments of kindness. Strangely, I now know how she feels.

At first, training Aero was a bit like that. If he did something right once, that was what gave me faith all the times he kept getting it wrong. You have to know that basically you're dealing with a good dog, or else you might feel pretty hopeless some days.

Mum knew that, despite all my temper tantrums, I was a good kid deep down.

'Watching you with Sophie, I could see what a caring, sensitive child you were – I knew you had a really big heart,' she told me years later, after she'd watched me with Aero, and could see how well we were both getting on together. 'Aero brings out the same side of you your sister did,' she added wisely, nodding her head almost to herself. Mum's read so much about ADHD on the Internet, she could probably become a doctor herself.

She knew about the wow factor.

Years later, a teacher of mine called Mr Blackmore spotted that wow factor too – again, much more of that presently. I'm getting ahead of myself (well, I do have ADHD).

But back then, when I was a five-year-old tearaway, we

didn't know I had a fancy disease, never mind a special factor to wow people with. And even though Mum had faith that I wasn't really a bad kid, it wasn't an opinion my teachers shared with her.

I started school at five, and instantly became known as a troublemaker.

'He's disruptive, rude and difficult to control,' was the general theme of my report cards and the frustrated phone calls from the school to my parents.

'Can you talk to him about his behaviour?' I'd overhear Mum asking Dad, exasperation dripping in her tired voice.

I can't remember what my first word was, but I'm pretty sure it was probably 'dunno'. When I got in from school, with my parents fresh off the phone from an angry teacher, I'd just shrug my shoulders and say, 'Dunno,' to Dad when he asked why I'd been naughty this time.

I suppose it was easier than trying to formulate words as to how I felt. Even then, I don't expect I could have mustered anything more enlightening than the D word. Truth is, I was as much a mystery to myself as I was to everyone else.

Back then, in those early days of learning about society and a world outside the confines of 'home', the classroom was like my best friend. I knew every corner of it by heart. Most days I'd do an entire lap of the place. I'd start out at the back – that was my preferred spot – where I could misbehave and lack concentration to my heart's content. Or, at least, for about ten minutes or so – some days even less. Inevitably it wouldn't be long before I'd blurted out something inappropriate, or upset someone, so I'd be pulled up to the front, the teacher demanding that I sit right in their eye-line, so that they could keep a very beady eye on me. Then, again rather predictably, I'd be ordered to stay in the classroom during playtime, usually for making crude and stupid comments in order to get laughs.

Such confinement was completely normal for me, and although being kept in a closed area was appalling for a kid with my condition, I accept that much of the time I'd brought it on myself. It was a no-win situation for the teachers. If they let me off the leash and into the playground, nine times out of ten I'd get into trouble – yes, nicking toys, hurting other kids (physically or verbally) – but keeping me securely indoors made me even more frustrated. I was like a caged beast, prowling up and down the room, watching the happy kids playing and enjoying themselves outside. They looked so alien to me. I wanted to be able to go and play and laugh with them, but I honestly didn't know how to get along with them. No one had ever welcomed me into their group, and no one else I knew behaved like me. I felt that I didn't belong.

So I'd either march up and down, or just sit there, on a cold plastic chair designed not for lanky kids like me, but small, cheerful children who got to enjoy their playtime properly. I must have cut quite a figure, sprawled across a wooden table, hands drumming, legs motoring, mind racing. The bad days were when it all got too much and I'd throw a chair, or kick a desk; the good days were when I'd become surly and aggressive towards people. There was no real in-between. I was either a swine or a rotter . . . often both.

Our classrooms were bustling with kids, overcrowded some might say, so I'd battle with the others for attention. At home I was used to Mum lavishing the spotlight on me, but up against a room full of brats I had my work cut out. And I really went for it.

'Liam! Liam! Liam! Liam! Liam, that's enough!'

Some days, my name would be yelled so many times it stopped making sense as a word – you know how if you repeat a word over and over it just becomes a noise? Oh, never mind.

Every day my teachers would scream themselves hoarse as I mindlessly created my trail of destruction. It wasn't long before I was used to their shouting too, so it started to wash over me. On the way home, thoughts would be buzzing in and out of my head as I dismantled some bushes, or scratched down the side of a car; even loud shouting voices couldn't penetrate my consciousness and stop me from continuing on my berserk and destructive path. Part of my brain – a very small section I must emphasize – would acknowledge that some kind of telling-off was taking place, but so what? When was I not getting a telling-off? It probably sounds really weird for anyone who hasn't experienced mental health problems, but the truth is that it didn't upset me. My ham-fisted attempts at apologies were often insincere and it was obvious. The world didn't much like me, and I didn't much like it.

The main problem back then, and now sometimes (I'm far from perfect), was that I love my mum, and my bad behaviour made her cry, made her sad. That was enough to make me aware that I needed to change. From time to time I'd do something to make her proud – often inadvertently and totally by accident – but I liked the way it felt when she smiled at me. For most of my childhood, she was the centre of my universe.

Unfortunately my delight at pleasing her didn't make me see the error of my ways. Not then anyway. And because I'd been billed as the 'naughty child' at school, I became the scapegoat for every scrap of trouble going. Which just made matters worse.

Every day was like a ticking time bomb, and it wasn't so much a question of whether I'd get into trouble, more of *when* I was going to get into trouble. Most days I'd spend morning break in the classroom, then I'd make it to the headmaster's office before lunch.

Some days I wouldn't even know why I was there. Trouble became a bit of a blur, like the red mist that everyone talks about descending. It was hard to pinpoint what would trigger my outbursts, but we've since come to the conclusion that they were mainly the result of the frustration of seeing the other kids socializing, or adapting to new surroundings, or understanding new lessons being taught, and feeling more and more stupid, because I was struggling so much with everything. Why couldn't I be as clever as them? Why wasn't I picking up things as easily as them?

'Come on, Liam, I'll need an answer,' my teacher would insist, tapping the blackboard impatiently. As usual I'd have spent the whole lesson blurting out the wrong answers to everyone else's questions, but once it was my turn, I would be overcome by a total inability to concentrate. I needed to be in a calm mood to survive a maths class. The numbers would be buzzing around on the page, never staying still for a minute, and there was no way in a million years that I'd be relaxed enough to figure it out.

It was frustrating, not just for the teachers, but for me too. I would have solved the puzzle if I could, and I really wanted to. I just couldn't. And, worse still, I couldn't explain why I found it so hard, so I'd find myself getting angry about the situation. And unfortunately, a lanky kid slamming down his fists on to a fragile wooden desk while screaming and shouting gets you to one place at school – the headmaster's office.

'Right, that's it, Liam, get out! The headmaster will be expecting you,' teachers would yell.

And off I would flounce; another day, another showdown with the boss.

The headmaster's office was the most petrifying place in the whole world. It was probably just a normal school office, like millions of others all over the world, but because I only went there in troublesome situations, it felt really spine-chilling. The minutes spent sitting outside awaiting my punishment – clearing chewing gum out of the playground, dreaded lines – were the longest, most painful minutes you could ever imagine. I'm sure each minute lasted at least ninety seconds on the clock outside his office, each tick and tock getting gradually slower and louder, as the tension and nerves grew steadily towards fever pitch. If I put together the hours I've spent either waiting nervously to see my headmaster, or sitting patiently in doctors' waiting rooms, I'd probably have at least a year extra to play with. And, as you can understand, waiting was not an ideal pastime for people with my illness. It could be agonizing.

'So what happened this time, Liam?' he would ask, peering over his glasses, his eyes burning with a quiet fury.

I would sit there, my feet rocking a few inches off the floor. I was one of the tallest kids in my class, but even so the seat in the headmaster's office was way too high for me. The rumour was that he did it on purpose to remind us that we were just tiny little people, and he was the real boss around here. His feet didn't seem to have any trouble touching the floor. They were rooted to the coarse red carpet that was worn down to the thinnest of layers after years of naughty children had dragged their feet defiantly through the office.

'I don't know, sir,' I would reply, looking down at my hands, doing all I could to avoid eye contact. That was always my trick back then: look glum, and for heaven's sake don't let them look you in the eye. I remember often feeling terrible about what I had done – whether I had upset one of my classmates, or, worse still, one of the teachers – but I didn't know how to explain it. I just didn't have the words, and my eyes often belied my guilt. I had what's known in the teaching trade as a 'cheeky glint' and unfortunately anything cheeky rarely comes across as sincere. What I wanted to do most at those times was to cry and say sorry, but I was so confused. I never meant to be bad or to get into trouble.

At the end of my first year at school I wasn't going back. Mum decided to send me somewhere else and see how I got on there.

Yeah, not very well, as it happens. No surprise there.

On the walk to school I'd pick up a stone and scrape it along the shiny doors of all the parked cars I walked past. In class I'd taken to making weird noises to disrupt the lesson. When the teacher told me to calm down and shut up, I'd swear back at him, looking around the class with a big goofy grin. Next I'd stamp my feet on the floor and make the strange noises again.

Not exactly your model student then. Plus I was getting older, and any charm or 'cheeky glint' was seriously starting to fade.

I was such a handful that the headmaster decided to exclude me during lunchtimes.

As in my first school, they'd tried keeping me in class when everyone else played, but that didn't work, and neither did granting me the responsibility of behaving myself. No chance. And thus I went home at lunchtime, which didn't seem so bad to me if I'm being honest, but it was a total nightmare for my mum who was at work half an hour away. Mum had to collect me from school while the exclusion lasted, and in despair – and on the advice of the school – she sent me to a child psychologist. They weren't much use though.

It was weird for all concerned, because the minute I arrived at their offices and started the session, I was fine. Well, not fine, but I reverted to being the same kind of character I was when I was in the headmaster's office trying to keep myself out of punishment's way. Or when my grandparents came over. I'd sit there, politely answering their questions. Like I was shy or something.

After a few sessions they signed me off and said Mum could cope. Mum kept going back, and taking me to different places too. But no one could get to the bottom of my behaviour.

Things went from bad to worse. At school I made friends, but I couldn't keep them. I'd kick off at the slightest provocation, punching and swearing. Not the kind of mate you'd want, really. Mum says that every day she'd get a call from the school and think, oh no, here we go again.

It wasn't a pretty picture inside my head either. It felt like me against the world. Nothing I did was good enough. It was like living in a puzzle where the pieces never fitted. I didn't realize it at the time, but looking back my self-esteem had taken a pretty big kicking too. You can only handle so much of being told you're a loser. Friends didn't want me, the school didn't want me, and eventually it felt like even Mum and Dad didn't want me. By the time I was eight, I think they were at their wits' end.

Then Mum got a call from a friend whose son had just been diagnosed with ADHD. 'I think your Liam's got it too,' she told her.

Mum put the phone down and went online straight away. As the search engine started to list websites dealing with this mystery illness, Mum knew she was on to something.

She read that it was a neurological condition (that's brain problem to you and me) that could be treated with medication, but couldn't be cured. Mr Google said it was like having an invisible disability, so it was hard for people to believe it was real.

Handily, a lot of the websites had a checklist of symptoms. I bet Mum almost fell off her chair when she read them: it was like reading my school report.

She called Dad into the room, and they looked at the list together in shock:

- Aggressive, prone to breaking things and injuring themselves
- Blurts out responses, often shouting out in class without being asked
- Impatient, and unable to stand in line or wait in turn
- Intrudes on others, often interrupting other people's conversations or games
- Unable to remain seated
- Runs and climbs excessively in inappropriate situations
- Talks excessively and fidgets
- Makes noise all the time, and is unable to play quietly

How did they know me so well? Had these web people been spying on me? It was uncanny! I went off to check the house for bugs and hidden cameras, and with me smashing around in the background, Mum continued to read that kids with ADHD were at their worst behaved in situations where there were lots of people around, and lots going on to get all revved up by. So classrooms, family gatherings and parties were like trouble hotspots. Uh-oh. Basically, any situation where it might probably be a good idea to pipe down and do as you were told was like a red rag to a bull for people with ADHD. Mum also read that in highly focused circumstances, like a one-on-one meeting with a psychologist, the symptoms might not show up. Which explains why when Mum had tried to get help before, they'd told her there wasn't anything much wrong with me. It's a slippery little fella, this ADHD.

The next day Mum called up the hospital and begged, 'You need to help me now.'

When she explained how bad my behaviour had got, they gave her an emergency appointment with a child psychologist.

Within weeks we were sitting in a hospital waiting room.

The doctor's office was the usual affair: uncomfortable chairs, old comics, Mum lost in *Woman's Own*. These places were like a second home to me – or third home if you count the classroom as my second one. Let's call them my 'holiday home', even if they were anything but warm and alluring. I'd been in and out of so many different doctors' offices and medical centres that receptionists would even say hello to me in the street. After most visits, Mum would drive me home in almost complete silence; or she'd be tutting and mumbling to herself, annoyed with whatever the doctor had thought necessary to say to her in private. I'd put on the radio to cheer her up. Sometimes we'd sing together, sometimes I'd sing a solo. I'm pretty rubbish with song lyrics, so I'd have to make them up.

But this time it was different. No private whispered chats, no welling up from Mum. I was included in all the conversations, and the doctor seemed really interested to know my thoughts on what might be wrong with me. I'd explained how I some-times felt like my mind was racing and how it could be hard to concentrate in class. Some teachers at school had told me that I was a 'problem child', I was 'abusive' or 'disruptive', but the doctor smiled and told me I was none of those things. He knew exactly what was wrong with me.

I looked over at Mum, who was smiling at me. This was definitely the first time she had looked so cheerful during one of these visits. Normally she'd be doing most of the talking, pleading with the doctor not to dismiss my problems as me just being naughty – she believed in me even if they didn't. She'd be using her stern voice. But now she wasn't doing any of the talking, and I was doing a lot of it. People were actually listening, looking like they were genuinely interested in what I had to say. It felt great.

Mum interrupted my chatter by asking, 'Is it ADHD?' in an urgent tone. Then added, 'I've read about it on the Internet, and I'm sure Liam's got it.' She spoke hesitantly, not wanting to tell the doctor how to do his job, but determined to mention it.

'Oh yes, without a doubt,' said the doctor, looking up and smiling as if it were the silliest question in the world.

And with those words eight years of head-scratching, buckets of tears, and a couple of different schools all began to make sense. It marked the beginning of a whole new life, where everything that had gone before wasn't down to me being a bad person. I was ill, but, weirdly, the future was bright. Of course, at the time I didn't get what a breakthrough it was. All I knew was that the doctor was being nice to me, and was listening to what I said rather than telling me to shut up, stop causing trouble and go and stand outside. He was better than a teacher, and nicer than the doctors who'd always stared straight through me.

My mum must have been so relieved finally to get some answers. Looking back, I realize how good my parents were about it all. I might have been behaving badly, but they weren't returning the favour. Sometimes Mum might get a little bit cross with me, but no more so than any parent would with their child. Now, sitting in that office, she was proud of me, and proud of herself for sticking with the mission to get to the bottom of this mystery.

I was still blabbing away, loving the attention. 'And sometimes

I just can't sit still. I want to but I can't, and sometimes I get really frustrated and I kick things, and sometimes . . .' This felt brilliant, and there was no way I was going to waste this positive attention.

Normally, the only time people listened to me was when I was standing in front of them, tail firmly between my legs, apologizing for the umpteenth time for something I had done to upset them. That could be any number of things, mainly destroying stuff (rose bushes, wing mirrors, brand-new toys), or upsetting their feelings somehow. They'd never make it easy for me, like I'd never made it easy for myself, but what those people didn't know was that every time I stood there, cap in hand, I really was sorry – genuinely sorry. I hated myself for my terrible behaviour, though sometimes I didn't even understand how or why I'd been bad.

Of course, at that time I didn't know I was ill, no one did. I'm not using that as an excuse. It's simply how it was. This was before we'd found a brilliant doctor with enough know-how to see that I wasn't just another naughty boy doing naughty things.

'The great news is that we do have some medication we can put you on right away, and you should see the results immediately, or at least in the first couple of weeks,' he said, putting a comforting hand on my mum's arm. He must have known what she'd been going through.

He scribbled down my prescription on a piece of paper in writing even worse than mine. I could make out the word Ritalin, but I hadn't a clue what it was.

Mum raced straight to the chemist, and within hours I'd popped my first pill (the first of many!) that would hopefully calm me down.

Twenty minutes after I'd taken it, Mum decided to test me. 'Please could you go upstairs and get my shoes, love?' she asked nervously.

I'd usually freak out if she asked me to do stuff like that, kicking doors and swearing. 'Okay, Mum,' I mumbled, running upstairs as I'd been asked.

Mum looked at me with wide eyes, and mouthed, 'Oh, my God.'

Then I scampered back to the living room to watch TV.

Mum tried again: 'Will you put the bread on the table for dinner, please?' she asked, smiling.

Asking me to do anything when I was watching TV was like pressing the nuclear button. I would normally go mental, and any breakable items nearby probably wouldn't survive my tantrum. I was that bad.

But instead, like a miracle on two gangly legs, I trotted off like an obedient pup to get the bread. For the first time in eight years, Mum could bring me to heel.

Later that night, she asked how I was feeling.

'My head's not fuzzing any more,' I told her, happily playing with my toys.

Mum hummed to herself, smiling as she made dinner for me and my brother and sister that night. The radio was playing down the charts, and we were singing along and dancing around the kitchen. I'd never seen her so happy; it was like a huge weight had been lifted from her shoulders – probably because that's exactly what had happened.

'He's not a bad boy at all!' she said with a smile, talking to my dad when he got home, relaying the information from the doctor. 'He's just a bit poorly. The doctor says it's not even unusual for boys his age to have problems with their concentration spans, and it's not him being lazy.'

Dad looked impressed, and gave me a playful little jab on the shoulder. 'Well, I knew that all along,' he joked.

'We were right,' went on Mum. 'He's got Attention Deficit Hyperactivity Disorder.' She beamed, as we all sat there cheerfully shovelling omelette, chips and beans into our mouths.

She winked at me, and ruffled my hair. I smiled in response, then went back to my chips.

The truth is that the name of my affliction was pretty much all we knew; not only that, it was all *anyone* knew. Even now, seven years after being diagnosed with ADHD, people are still arguing about what it is exactly, and, more importantly, how people get it. The symptoms are pretty universal and easy to spot – an inability to concentrate, periods of hyperactivity, mood swings and aggression. Whether it's genetic or avoidable is still being debated by clever men with numerous qualifications and posh voices. My feeling is that it lurks in the genes, and is probably unavoidable. In fact, the more we have learned about it, the more Mum is convinced that she may have suffered from it too when she was young.

Back in the early days of ADHD, when it was still being investigated, none of the medics we visited even mentioned it as a possibility to explain my behaviour. They listened, nodded, occasionally looked at me like I should perhaps be locked up, but not once did anyone utter the word 'hyperactive' (let alone 'attention deficit'); instead they used 'energetic' or 'restless' or just plain 'naughty'. But I don't blame anyone for not spotting what was really wrong with me; after all, it took a brilliant child psychologist, not a plain medicine man, to figure out that not all my misdemeanours stemmed from a desire to misbehave on purpose.

Being a 'disorder' made it sound really posh, we all agreed – not just an everyday problem, but an actual disorder. I think Mum liked that. I know I did. And for once I was looking forward to going to school just so that I could tell people I was poorly.

'Morning, Liam.'

'Morning, miss. I've got ADHD!' I chirped.

'I beg your pardon?'

And off I skipped down the corridor on my way to another boring maths lesson, hoping that my new medication was going to be as effective as promised.

Life at school was pretty bad, so I hoped this could turn it around. Staying out of trouble was hard, because my illness meant that I had all the symptoms of a bad student – shouting out comments on impulse, being disruptive and barely able to concentrate. But I could cope with the teachers thinking I was a right royal pain in the neck. Losing friends was the hard bit. A few mates stuck by me through all the ups and downs, but I've lost count of the others who have fallen by the wayside. People need to be patient with me, but I can't blame the ones who weren't. I wasn't the easiest kid to get along with. I was blacklisted from a lot of houses in the neighbourhood.

I've lost count of the times Mum had to sit me down to talk me through my latest misdemeanour, and she'd explain that I wouldn't be able to go to Stevie's or Tommy's or Spike's for a while – at least until their mums could trust me again. I'd have broken something – at the last count it was about ten plates, three vases and one portable radio – or had a screaming tantrum. I suppose I'd just act at other people's houses as I did at my own, and I didn't realize quite what a bad idea that was! I could never fathom what Mum meant at the time. One of the blessings of ADHD is that you move on from situations pretty fast.

Apart from the obvious behaviour issues, another problem causing big chunks of damage to our daily life was that I needed Mum's attention 24/7. My dad (Barry to his friends) was constantly working to make ends meet – as a driver – so when he wasn't around Mum had her hands full. This would have been slightly easier had it not been for Mathew and Sophie. Whenever Mum wasn't giving me her undivided attention, I'd start taking the house to bits, or screaming and crying until I was her focus again. This would result in more 'talks' about right and wrong – talks that seemed to go in one ear and out of the other.

Even so, while I was busy being the world's most annoying brat, Mum never stopped fighting my corner, and I know that there were times when she was at school more than me! She laughs about it now, but I'm sure that it was probably really stressful.

Mum tried everything to make me well – pleading with the teachers to be kinder to me, showering me with affection. Years before everyone started going bananas about school dinners and organic food, Mum had already taken it upon herself to put me on a special diet to help curb my bad behaviour. So that meant as few E numbers and artificial colours as possible. And it worked up to a point, especially knocking fizzy drinks on the head; that stuff for me was like rocket fuel, and even now if I have half a can I start getting a little bit manic. But, needless to say, it wasn't the miracle cure everyone was hoping for. I still spent the majority of each school day as the proud resident of the nearest 'naughty corner'.

In fact I'd become so used to sitting in naughty corners that I even created one of my own at home. Mum always laughs when she tells the story of me breaking a really nice vase that Dad had bought her for Valentine's Day. Apparently she heard a smash, hotfooted it into the lounge, only to find me sitting in the corner of the room facing the wall, explaining that I was sorry about the vase, and I'd spend the rest of the day in the naughty corner as punishment.

'I think you managed about five minutes, then you were off again!'

But, unfortunately, we don't look back and laugh at all of it. Obviously, being a kid and being told constantly that what you're doing is wrong can make you lose a lot of confidence around other children, and I became quite shy of people. I'd often feel awkward in situations. Some of the other children were a bit scared of me, and some plain just didn't like me, which was fair enough, given that there were times when I was pretty hard to like, because I didn't know how to play fairly. That feeling of being different to everyone else has, predictably, followed me into my teenage life. It had to, I suppose, and even now I can find perfectly normal social situations pretty daunting.

I'll admit it, I was really lonely. No one much wanted to hang out with me. If they pitied me from afar, they would quickly stop feeling sorry for me once I'd opened my mouth and snarled a mean comment at them. That happened a lot. A kid at school would see me not playing with anyone, probably destroying something, and their good nature and curiosity would bring them waddling over to see if I wanted to play. Skip the next minute or so, and they'd be sniffling beside a teacher, pointing at me, their sobs getting more exaggerated as they explained what I had just said or done. As with trained animals, the more this happened, the more the kids understood that it wasn't worth bothering to try next time. In fact, the next times became fewer and further between, until I was pretty much guaranteed as much alone time as I wanted. Even some of the teachers had stopped making the effort to speak to me. What they didn't know was that I was so sad, so alone, and so pining for someone to play with. I just didn't know how to ask.

Predictably, as I grew older and bigger in size, so did my peers and from time to time our crossed swords would take on a slightly more physical aspect. Unfortunately I'm an absolutely appalling fighter – ridiculously, for someone so used to rubbing people up the wrong way. I just have no technique. My limbs are long and my hands and feet are both oversized and relatively useless. I don't so much punch as waft at people, so most of the scrapes I have been in have resulted in me being on the losing team. But don't get the wrong idea about me. I don't like fights, in fact I positively hate them and do all in my power to avoid them. It's just that back then I had a bad reputation, and some of the harder kids at school liked the idea of taking me down a notch. What they didn't know was that there really wasn't any need, I was already down about a million notches. On the outside I might have come across as hardened, mean and street tough, although I was anything but.

Hence, these days, if I'm watching a film I'm always rooting for the bad guy, mainly because I sympathize with people who are seen as nasty. I can relate to them. When I was at my worst – no medication, no diagnosed condition to speak of – people were scared of me like I was Darth Vader. But deep down I knew there was a nice guy in there trying to get out. And, yes, that refers both to me and Lord Vader. He turned out okay.

Of course, I'd love to say that we'd found the miracle cure to all my problems when the drugs came along, but it wasn't that simple. What we had found was hope, the beginning of a longer journey to a better life. My manic episodes became less frequent, and I think because we knew that they were caused by my illness, it made them easier for us all to take.

Even so, the process of taking drugs was a strange one. It was like admitting that I wasn't normal, which I know I wasn't. But there were times during that early stage of medication when I'd become so sad and upset, I'd cry. It felt so unfair that the other kids could run around and play and be merry, while I had to take these nasty-tasting tablets just to feel almost okay. I was probably too young to be self-indulgent and overly self-pitying, but it separated me even more from the people around me. They didn't need any pills to stop them acting up, they were quite capable. It was fantastic and a massive relief for the family that we finally had this diagnosis, and could begin to make sense of my behaviour, but at the same time it pushed me a little bit further away from normal society. People knew I had a problem, and in some ways that made me easier to avoid. After all, if you were a parent, and your kid wanted to bring an ADHD friend around for tea, would you jump at the chance? No, neither would most of our neighbours. So, I stayed lonely. I often locked myself away in the shed to draw or muttered to myself like a loony. Some days I'd deliberately walk down the street talking loudly to myself, just for the fun of it. It's pretty hard to find entertainment when you've got no money and no pals.

After a while the Ritalin seemed to stop working for me; even taking it three times a day I'd be bouncing off the walls by the evening. Another huge problem was that my then school wasn't legally allowed to administer my medication, so there were days when I'd have to miss my dose. Those days were tough ones. Now I take a drug called Concerta, which I have done since I was about ten. Funnily enough, for all the facts and figures I struggled with on a daily basis at school, I know an unhealthy amount about prescription drugs and what they do.

Concerta is what they call a sustained-release tablet, which means that over the course of the day it will steadily release the chemicals I need to stay calm and mellow into my system drip by drip – it's a slow-burner. My routine now is that I take one in the morning, one at lunchtime and one in the evening (when I was at school I went to the nurse who administered the one at midday).

Without it I'd be like a jumping frog with a temper.

Even so, my behaviour wasn't the best. Situations that would start as usual childish banter would often escalate into big over-the-top rows, mainly because I didn't have that off button in my head that knew when to stop. The drugs added an element of control to my life, but they were by no means a cure for my condition. From around eight years old to fifteen I stumbled through life trying to find things to distract my mind. But nothing really worked.

2

Fame comes knocking, I answer

'I want a dog,' I pleaded with Mum, turning my voice up to the loud whine setting. 'Pleeeeeaaaaase!'

'Smells Like Teen Spirit' was playing in my room, and the loud racket was zinging round the house through the bedroom door I'd deliberately left open. Evenings at home were so boring that I liked to create the effect of a stadium concert bouncing off my four walls.

Mum's face looked like a painting of pain and total frustration all mixed up together. She wasn't much of a fan of decent grunge music, weirdly.

'Turn the music down. I've told you, we're not getting a dog.'

I kicked the skirting board hard, so my big toe really hurt through my trainers, then stalked back into my room, switching the music up to the highest volume. I'd got a cheap stereo, so it didn't have quite the effect I'd hoped, it just went really distorted, and even my hard-rock ears threatened to start bleeding. Still, it proved a point. Kind of.

Smokey, our old cat, lay on the bed, and looked up at me with mournful eyes. Nirvana wasn't one of his all-time favourites either, he was more of an easy listening-type cat. His ears flattened out and he curled his head into his paws giving me one long, withering look.

'Sorry,' I said, flopping on the bed and stroking his soft black fur. He looked like he'd understood what I'd said to Mum about wanting a dog and was upset; they say cats are very per-

28

ceptive, and Smokey occasionally had the look of a cat that had seen too much. Either that or Kurt Cobain was finally getting to him. But animals don't hold on to rock star grudges for long. As I tickled behind his ears, he started to purr and lick my hand. Smokey was a soppy old thing who smelled of cat biscuits, and I loved him. But I still wanted a dog. Unfortunately I lived in a house of cat lovers.

'Who'll look after him?' Mum always asked, her eyebrows raised into an accusing arch. 'Your dad and I haven't got time to take a dog for walks, and think of poor Smokey, Liam.'

'I will!' I'd bellow over my shoulder on my way back up the stairs in an offended tone. I knew what she was getting at.

I *really, really* wanted a dog. Someone to talk to, play with, take for walks. But Mum was worried about how little Smokey would react, especially as the cat was only a year younger than me, which in cat years is probably about a million years old. It was a fair point, I suppose, but it still annoyed me. In my heart I knew she was right. Smokey was scared enough of dogs barking in the distance, let alone in the house. Plus my attention span was shorter than a goldfish with concussion, so I probably wouldn't make the best dog owner. I was taking my medication, but it helped me cope with my condition, rather than cancelling it out. I'd start on some activity full of good intentions, then get distracted or bored and move on to another in a jiffy. Like, say, smashing something up. No dog needs to see that.

But would I be the same with a dog? I wasn't sure, and I could see why it was unfair to find out. But still, sitting in my bedroom, bored, with a mangy old cat whose only interests in life were sleeping and eating biscuits, it was hard to feel that there wasn't a conspiracy against me, with the whole world on the other team.

I made do by drawing a picture of a dog, paying close atten-tion to every scruff of fur. I inventively called it 'Dog'.

I was good at art, especially cartoons. Since the age of eight

I'd discovered that once I had a pen and paper in my hand the buzzing in my head bottomed out for a bit, and I'd get lost in drawing. What I like to call an 'art attack'. I doodled whatever I could see. I wasn't fussy; anything from a vase of flowers in the house, to a banana resting against an apple in the fruit bowl was fair game for me. Once, from memory, I drew a picture of some daffodils in a big metal bin. It was like my relationship with animals and babies: I liked stuff that couldn't talk back and tell me off.

Smokey closed his eyes, soothed by my tickles, and fell asleep. I hunched over my desk, doodling dogs with a determined look on my face. I could hear Mum and Dad rumbling around downstairs, making their way to bed. They were just glad I was in my room and not causing trouble.

'Night, Liam.' Mum poked her head round the door, and tried to give me a goodnight kiss.

'Eurggh,' I said ungratefully, wiping the side of my cheek.

I'd been in trouble at school. Again. I'd been sent out of maths class for swearing at the teacher. Honestly, it just pops out of my mouth. I somehow can't control my words.

Mum always insists that, unlike me, she absolutely loved going into class each day. She says she had a thirst for knowledge. I didn't inherit that. It must skip a generation, I would joke. No one else has ever really laughed at that one.

Ignoring my rude obliteration of her kiss, Mum gave a cheery wave and, as she left my room, Smokey followed her to settle down for the night on her bed. Mum and Dad didn't fidget as much as me.

I was dreading school the next day. The only person who kept me going was my head of year, Mr Blackmore. For some reason he'd taken a shine to me.

Only last week I'd been in his office. The papers on his desk were stacked in a massive pile, and every time he spoke I was sure they'd fall off. His short black hair was styled into quite a severe cut, and he looked every inch the strict teacher. But his eyes were softer. They reminded me of the warm expression I later recognized in Aero's eyes.

'If you're not going to turn things around you're going to jeopardize everything,' Mr Blackmore had said, fixing his eyes on me for a reaction. He twirled his pen in his hand as he waited for an answer.

I huffed as usual, slumped in the chair in my pea-green school uniform, with the tightest knot possible in my tie – impossible to undo, even to this day. I must have looked like a nightmare teenager, my lip curling with the unfairness of it all.

And yet Mr Blackmore somehow tolerated having a grumbling man-child in his office, making few apologies for yet more appalling behaviour. 'Liam, both of us know that you have the ability to do well, but I need to see you channel your energy into your work.'

'Yeah, whatever.'

And, with that, I lurched from my seat and down the corridor, my limbs shifting heavily, as if moments away from crumbling on to the floor with the boredom of it all. I was a typical teenager, and make no mistake.

As you can probably tell, by my mid-teens I was still having problems. When the medicine arrived, we'd hoped for an end to the trouble, but unfortunately it wasn't like that at all. In some ways matters had grown worse. After all, a cute little terror misbehaving is easier to forgive than a lanky teenager with a voice that is deep one minute and squeaky the next. My outbursts had lost their charm and innocence, and the older I got, the more of a misfit I felt. I was still very disruptive in class, a potent cocktail of teenage hormones and faulty neurotransmitters in my head which were barely held at bay by the drugs, bravely fighting a losing battle. But, like Mum says, who knows how bad it could have been if I hadn't had a loving family and a diagnosis backed up with drugs? But the fact was, even though I wasn't someone the police might want in connection with a number of crimes, neither was I the kind of person a school would want, messing around and creating chaos in its classrooms.

Luckily, Mr Blackmore knew all this and still believed in me. Somehow (and God knows how) he'd seen through to my wow factor.

'You have the potential to turn this around, you really do,' he had told me earnestly the week before, after my latest spot of bother.

I suddenly realized I was on a motorway to a very bad place and Mr Blackmore had just shown me where the last exit was.

I knew things were going down the pan. Recently I'd moved my troublemaking up a peg or two. I'd always been considered the class clown, a bit of a cheeky chappy, but unfortunately my behaviour had started to boil over into bullying, and, being taller than most of the other kids at school – roughly the same height as a professional basketball player or a small tree – I suppose I made for quite a threatening sight. I'd also developed a very silly habit of being abusive to my teachers. I'd lost count of the times I'd been sent home from school for being bad, and detention wasn't really a punishment any more, it was just part of my normal timetable. Mr Blackmore was trying to warn me that if I didn't shape up, there wasn't much more he could do for me.

But then fate popped a dog-shaped gift in his lap. Could this save me?

There was no real indication that this week would be any different. I loped into school, listening to banging music on my headphones, with a weird unsettled feeling in my stomach. I was at that age when the teachers keep urging you to 'think about the future'. But when I looked ahead it seemed pretty dark out there.

As I strolled down the corridor, in no rush to make the class I was late for, Mr Blackmore stopped me and said, 'Liam, can I have a word?'

Something in his manner was different though. He was a nice bloke, but even so I wasn't used to such a calm tone of voice. Normally we were on surname terms, and his face seemed much softer than usual too. Teachers can look so . . . human, I thought.

'What for, sir?'

'I have something I want to talk to you about.'

I set myself a surly look, expecting to be told off, or sent to the headmaster to explain why I had upset yet another class-mate. But nothing came, or at least there wasn't any telling-off. I could still hear the din of kids scuttling past on their way to wherever they were going – I wasn't yet in the eye of the storm. I had to pinch myself. Twice.

'Come on, come to my office, Liam.'

I moped behind him all the way along the bustling corridor, limbs loose like a monkey carrying a log. I must have behaved really badly to warrant Mr Blackmore coming all the way out of his office to find me, only to take me back to his office. There must be a firing squad in there, I thought. Or, worse still, Mum and Dad had been called in and I was totally done for.

'Sit down, Liam.'

I folded myself into a chair, and deflated into it like a leaking balloon.

'I'm putting you forward for a TV show.'

What! I suddenly sat upwards, my eyebrows rocketing right to the top of my forehead, like they were trying to kiss my hairline. This was a turn-up for the books, to say the least.

'Come again, sir?'

'I'm serious, Liam. The BBC is making a documentary, and I've recommended you be put forward for it.'

Wow, a documentary. A serious, hard-hitting take on the world of Liam Creed. What a fantastic idea, I thought. In my wildest dreams I'd always imagined being a TV star, but now it was actually happening. This sounded very interesting indeed.

'What, so I'll really be on telly?' I asked, wiping my nose

with my sleeve just to show how incredulous I was. Stuff like this doesn't happen to kids like *me*, I told myself. The weird thing was, even though I could be cripplingly shy in real life, the thought of appearing on TV, in front of millions of people, didn't bother me. I'd spent my life feeling like a worthless nobody – this was my chance to be a proper *celebrity*. I silently chewed that word round my mouth like the best macaroni cheese ever, and mentally booked in my photoshoot with *OK!* magazine. I'd probably even wash my hair for it. As thoughts of my impending worldwide fame swirled round my head, Mr Blackmore's voice broke through the fog of my glittery daydreams about private jets and the cream of Hollywood's finest womenfolk clearing a bedside spot for me.

'Don't you even want to know what it's about?' he asked, leaning back in his chair in quiet exasperation.

'Oh, yeah.' Actually, I suddenly thought, this is a wind-up. After all, what had I, a lanky teenager from Chichester, got to offer anyone? Let alone people on a telly programme.

'You'll be training dogs,' Mr Blackmore said, folding his arms.

The Tinseltown beauty slipped from my arms, but the thought of something much cuddlier replaced her. Perhaps a soap actress.

'Dogs?' I repeated stupidly, my mind casting back to the picture I'd been working on the night before. Wow. Someone, beardy bloke in the sky or whoever, had finally answered my prayers. Mum wouldn't let me have a dog – but here was one about to woof his way into my life. I was so excited on hearing the D word I even forgot about my impending fame.

'Yes, dogs. But this is not some walk in the park, if you forgive the pun,' he added, standing up to find a leaflet from his bookshelves. 'This is really serious. It's helping a charity called Canine Partners train very special dogs to help disabled people have a better quality of life,' he informed me, passing me a newsletter from the charity, which had loads of information alongside pictures of happy-looking dogs wearing tabards announcing that they were on an important mission.

'Oh,' I replied, a little bit gobsmacked. It sounded like hard work, and I suddenly worried whether I would be up to the job. Not that I let Mr Blackmore see this. 'So what's this got to do with me? I've never had a dog – why would they want me to help train them?' I asked, confused by it all.

Mr Blackmore cleared his throat nervously and shuffled his feet on the floor. 'It's TV, Liam . . . you know, reality TV. They want to put kids with, um, problems on the show to see how they cope, and if working with the dogs helps them deal with their problems too . . .' He trailed off, a bit embarrassed to admit that my big chance had come along because I was a nightmare student.

Then it started to dawn on me . . . *They wanted to train me too.* Everything else had failed. This was the only option they could think of now. With millions watching me if I cocked it up. But even I, with some wounded pride, could see it was a brilliant opportunity.

'If you're interested, Liam, it will last three months and you'll take a day off school a week to attend training sessions at the Canine Partners dog centre, out in the countryside.'

My eyes lit up again. Dogs. Get out of school. Could this get any better?

His face suddenly grew stern, just like I remembered it from our fiercer discussions. 'So you'll need to commit one hundred per cent to this, no slacking.'

'Of course, no problem,' I said, the words coming out far more sarcastically than I'd intended.

'I'm serious, Liam, this is a big undertaking, and you won't just be there representing yourself, you'll be representing the whole school. I have to trust you on this.'

'But they want troubled teens, sir. I will be as troubled as I can.'

'Don't be cheeky, Liam.'

'I'm sorry,' I said, genuinely, aware that I should probably curb my wisecracks for a bit. This sounded like a great opportunity, and I really didn't want to blow it.

'Four other kids will be on the course with you, all from different schools in the area, but all a similar age.'

I felt myself burn up a bit. I wasn't going to mention it in that room to Mr Blackmore, but new people scared me a little. Especially new people my age. As outlined already, one skill I hadn't learned growing up was how to be sociable and how to interact naturally with people my age. If there were going to be girls there, I was guaranteed to go into total meltdown. My school was boys only, and, although I enjoyed female company for the most part, I didn't have much experience of girls my age. I found them confusing, with their made-up faces and strange-smelling perfumes, and nice silky clothes. Who were they? Who did they think they were? Plus, I hate to admit it, but I wasn't the smoothest guy in the world.

'Oh, right, cool, sounds great, really excellent.' I nodded, trying to hold it together. 'Do we know who the other kids are?'

'No, but needless to say they'll have their fair share of, um, troubles too.'

'Righty-ho.' I chuckled. Mr Blackmore had a funny way of putting things – troubles. Brilliant.

I looked down at the pamphlet and glanced at the pictures. They were all of dogs and people in wheelchairs – the dogs looked terrific. I didn't know a great deal about types of dog, but I knew a Labrador when I saw one. They always look like they're smiling, which is cool. I would love to say that I read the pamphlet, but I don't have the greatest concentration span, so it probably took me a few weeks finally to get through to the end. I'd often start reading it, but I'd be easily distracted by whatever was going on around me. With three kids and a whole host of friends and neighbours coming in and out, my house isn't the quietest place in the world. And that's exactly how we like it.

'It looks excellent, sir.' I smiled, pretending to peruse the pamphlet, but, um, not. 'I promise to take it seriously, and I won't let you down.'

'Remember this is your last chance to make something of yourself, not just an opportunity to skive,' he warned me. But I could see his eyes were smiling. 'Oh, and I'll need to get your parents' permission. If you have a chat with them tonight, I'll call tomorrow.'

My smile faded, like someone had bent the corners downwards. What if they refused? I *had* to persuade them.

I walked out feeling like a new person. Suddenly I had a purpose in life. A four-legged future loomed over me, rather than a dark, ominous cloud.

I was going to be a famous dog handler, like that girl with the dancing dog on *Britain's Got Talent*. This must be how Kurt Cobain felt when he got his first breakthrough gig. It was rock'n'roll with dog treats.

The day whizzed by on a cloud of my unbearable smugness. By the time I got home, my chirpiness was bordering on insanity.

'Well, good evening, Mr Cheerful!' Mum greeted me, looking puzzled.

I'd bounced in whistling. As I've previously described, I didn't tend to return home feeling so good. But tonight I was in the best mood ever. Life had never felt so rosy.

'I've got big news, Mum!' I said, slinging my bag on to the sofa, and standing proudly in the middle of the lounge. 'I am going to be ON TELEVISION!'

'Oh, stop it!' Mum laughed, wafting the idea away with her hand.

'I'm serious.'

I explained how Mr Blackmore had put me forward to help out at a dog-training centre, and there was going to be a camera crew and everything. Mum looked really impressed, and it wasn't long before we were both leaping up and down in the living room like total maniacs.

'Our Liam . . . on TV . . . training dogs . . .' Mum kept mouthing the words to herself as if Jesus had just popped by to perform a minor miracle. Thankfully we'd calmed down and resumed normal levels of excitement by the time Dad returned home from a long day behind the wheel.

We had to persuade him it was a good idea too, and he wasn't as easy to impress.

'A TV show, huh?' Dad slurped his tea. 'What about?'

'It's on the BBC,' I said, looking for approval (as everyone knows the BBC is very hoity-toity). 'Um, it's about a dog school thing . . . and, erm, they want kids with problems . . .'

The last word hung in the air. He looked at me sharply. 'Hang on, kids with problems? I'm not having us made to look like freaks for the sake of some TV show.'

He had a good point. I'd made letting people down my speciality. Why was this any different? And the stakes were much, much higher. Mum and Dad could be totally humiliated in front of their neighbours, friends and colleagues. The problem with ADHD was that it was easy to point the finger of blame at the parents.

If I freaked out on TV, it wouldn't just be me who was shown up. People would start to talk, and say that we must be a problem family. People would presume I hadn't been brought up properly, and wouldn't realize I had a posh disorder stuffed in my genetic pocket that meant I was hardwired to misbehave. It was a big risk.

Mum looked at Dad, expectantly, the earlier gleam of hope in her eyes starting to fade. Then she said firmly, 'I think it's a good idea, and it'll do Liam the world of good.' She threw the comment at Dad like a grenade. 'You know how good he is with kids and animals,' she added in a softer tone. 'If he can succeed at anything, then surely it's this . . .'

Dad sighed, not totally convinced by the argument. I guess he was weighing it all up. He knew I was on a fast track to nowhere and this could be the turning point for me. But equally it could all blow up in our faces.

'Let me think about it,' he said, looking at our excited expressions. 'I want to speak to this Mr Blackmore before I make my mind up,' he stated with a finality that declared the debate was over – for now.

I went to bed feeling a pick-'n'-mix of emotions. On the one hand I was excited beyond belief, then nervous Dad would say no, then even *more* nervous he would say yes, but that I'd blow it and prove everyone right, that I was a total failure.

The last thing I saw before I went to sleep was my doodle of a dog staring back at me from my desk. What would my dog be like? I wondered as I drifted off into visions of one man and his mutt, of us scampering off into the sunset.

The next day, Mum and I sat pensively by the phone waiting for it to ring. I'd had a word with Mr Blackmore, saying how keen my mum was, but that my dad still needed a bit of persuading. 'I'll see what I can do,' he'd told me with a grin.

So here we were, waiting for the phone to ring, while Dad was lost in his newspaper.

Mum picked up the phone before the first ring could even travel as far as Dad's chair in the living room. 'Hello, I'm Liam's mum,' she said proudly. This was probably the first time she'd spoken to someone from the school about anything positive.

They had a quick chat, and then she called Dad over.

'Right then, what's all this about?' he boomed into the phone.

We watched as he nodded in silence at what Mr Blackmore was saying, punctuated with him repeating words like 'opportunity' and 'last chance'. It was almost impossible to read what Dad was thinking as he was on the phone. I was, of course, hoping that he knew how much this meant to me. It's all

I'd been thinking about for the last couple of days, which in ADHD terms is the equivalent of about a year. I don't think my brain had stayed so intensely focused on a single topic – probably ever. This was mega-important. I felt a bit like one of those contestants on big singing talent shows awaiting the verdict. What was the public vote going to say? Would Liam Creed be going through to the next round? After fifteen years of toil, hardship and bad run of luck after bad run of luck, in my mind I was due a silver lining. My eyes were pleading with Dad to read my mind and understand that this was by far the right thing to do, while I crossed just about all my fingers and toes.

Finally, he put down the phone and looked thoughtful for a moment. Both Mum's and my faces fell below ground level. Probably lower. I could practically hear my heart beating through my top.

'Well?' I squealed, a little too high-pitched.

Dad didn't say a word. He just looked serious and thoughtful.

'Oh, come on, darling, put us out of our misery,' said Mum, squeezing my hand.

Suddenly he beamed, broke into the world's biggest grin and said, 'Oh, what the hell, if your mum thinks it's okay, you can do it. It sounds like a fantastic show.'

I flung my arms around him. He gave me a big bear hug back.

'Just make sure they make us look good, okay?' he said.

Mum smiled at me excitedly. We were going to take the world by storm.

'So what exactly will Liam be doing?' asked Mum, after we'd all calmed down a bit. Attention to detail isn't one of my gifts – particularly when I'm over-excited – so I hadn't been able to give everyone the fullest account of what Mr Blackmore had told me the day before.

Sitting back down in his armchair, Dad explained what he'd

been told, with me and Mum as captive audience on the sofa, joined by Sophie who wanted to know all about it too.

'Liam's gonna be on a TV.' She kept giggling, giving me a sharp nudge in the side with her elbow. If I could cope with a kid sister, a pup would be easy work, I thought, scowling as I tried to listen to Dad.

According to Mr Blackmore, Canine Partners was a dog school, where a crew of highly dedicated experts teach puppies to go out into the real world to help disabled people with their day-to-day lives. Like most people, I'd heard of guide dogs for blind people, but I had to get this one explained a few times before it really sank in. The dogs spent a year living with 'puppy parents' – based all round the country – who took them to training sessions one day a week. During this year the dogs learned how to fit in with family life, and how to get along with other people. At fourteen months old they graduated to the Canine Partners training centre where the real hard work began. These dogs were trained to answer phones, go shopping, call lifts – all sorts of wonderful tasks. It sounded fascinating. And a bit weird.

'How can a dog answer a phone?' I grumbled to myself, thinking how bonkers it sounded. I'd imagined me and my pooch mucking about in fields, not fiddling with washing machines and the like. Eventually, Dad carried on explaining, after three months' intensive training, the dogs were placed with a disabled person, and went to live in their home. The dogs were a massive help in lots of practical ways, and they were also a great friend to people who could get lonely and depressed.

I'll be honest, at this point in my life I'd never known a disabled person, so it was hard for me to understand the difficulties they faced on a day-to-day basis. But I did understand the loneliness, so I could relate to them in that sense. It's horrible not feeling like there's anyone out there fighting your corner. I knew I had my family, but I always saw it as their job to accept me – 'unconditional love' and all that. After all, I forgave them all their bad habits too. But there were days when I wanted more than a Creed family member to knock around with, I wanted a companion to chat to.

ADHD sufferers aren't known for being big on the whole empathy thing. So even though it was a great opportunity to help change someone *else's* life, all I could think about was the bits that would be good for me. Namely having a dog and being a celebrity. Shamefully shallow, I know. But sadly that's how I was.

The next day, for probably the first time ever, I arrived at school in a great mood, feeling a million feet tall all of a sudden.

'Thank you, fans, no autographs please!' I joked, walking into class.

The rumour had already got out that I was going to be on telly, and people were looking at me with new-found respect. Being a future television star gave me a cool aura that I'd been after for years. I couldn't believe my luck.

Of course, to make it sound extra special, I'd slightly exaggerated what it was all about.

'So what is it?'

'It's about me!' I'd insist. 'The BBC wanted a kid to star in a show about dog training, and I got the gig.'

I leaned back in my chair, and put my feet on the desk, almost immediately getting my comeuppance when I nearly fell off the chair. I put a hand down to save myself from any shame, and composed myself. Note to self: don't attempt to pull off cool poses, you're just not that kind of guy.

'But what do you know about training dogs, Creed?'

'More than you,' I would lie, 'more than you.'

I enjoyed alluding to some kind of extra-curricular skill with dogs that no one knew about. To my mind, it made me seem exciting and fascinating. In actuality, I think everyone knew I was talking it up. Especially when I'd start dodging their simple questions about types of dogs and so on. The truth is, even though I'd wanted a dog for so long, I knew practically nothing about them.

I had always felt like such a thickie at school though, and would find myself watching as the other kids enjoyed treats as a reward for their hard work. I'd developed a knee-jerk hatred of high achievers, because it felt like nothing positive was ever going to happen to me. So while it was probably a bit idiotic of me to make such a big deal of a television show that hadn't taken place yet, and wasn't exactly about me, part of me realized that I just wanted to know what it felt like to be one of those lucky, hard-working kids who had good things happen to them. I must admit, even at that stage, before the filming had begun, the idea of taking up an activity that sounded interesting and unusual was intoxicating. Some part of me, hidden back in the depths of my subconscious, liked the notion of being really good at something that not everyone else could do. Whatever it was that Mr Blackmore could see in me that was worth persevering with, I think secretly I could see it too. I hadn't given up on me either.

That night I curled up next to Smokey, and wondered what I'd got myself into. Dogs seemed somehow a lot more human than cats. Smokey just lounged about, sleeping, purring and eating. We were great pals, no doubt about it, but I'm not sure Smokey would really miss me if I wasn't there chatting away to him most evenings. You just didn't have to *do* anything with him. Dogs were a different kettle of fleas. They weren't content with a comfy bed and a full food bowl. They wanted to be friends, *proper friends*. They liked to take you on walks, and be there by your side at all times. They were pack animals who considered themselves part of a team – *your* team. That was a lot of pressure for a loner like me. I didn't have friends like that – not the kind who wanted to knock around with me all the time and would put themselves on the line in a fight for me. I was used to it being me against the world. I wasn't sure I was ready to let anyone else in. Not even a dog.

I decided to do some research. I think my mum almost fell over from the shock of me using the computer for something other than playing pointless games. I could see her give Dad a knowing look, as if to say, 'Told you so, he's changing already.'

From reading the leaflet Mr Blackmore had given me I knew that most of the dogs at Canine Partners were golden retrievers, Labradors or a mix of both, although my knowledge didn't extend much beyond their names. This choice of breeds wasn't just a happy coincidence either. It was deliberate. They were the best dogs for the job in hand.

'Aren't they the dogs that wrap themselves up in loo roll?' Sophie asked, snorting with laughter, bringing a smirk to my older brother Mathew's face.

As you can imagine, I wasn't exactly the best brother in the world, and even though they were pleased I was getting a chance to sort myself out, they couldn't help poking fun at me. 'Oi, Andrex man,' sniggered my brother, joining in.

'Yeah, yeah, yeah,' I replied, waving them away dismissively with my hand. 'Very funny. I think you'll find that Labradors are actually the most popular dogs in the world,' I added, looking through the information I'd downloaded. Plus, anyway, what was so wrong with the puppies in the Andrex ads? Was I the only person in the country to find them cute and alluring? I think probably not.

I squinted and looked closer at the words in front of me describing Labradors as gentle, intelligent and good-natured. But that wasn't what had caught my attention.

A sentence further down had pinged out at me, and almost poked me in the eye.

These dogs are food- and fun-orientated and can be boisterous if not trained.

Whoa there. This was my kind of dog. Literally. Food, fun and frolicking around sounded like three major interests I could get seriously into.

I read on, an intent, interested look replacing my trademark surly expression.

Labradors mature at around three years of age; before this time they can have a significant degree of puppyish energy, often mislabelled as being hyperactive. Because of their enthusiasm, leash-training is suggested early on.

The words hung in my mind like a graffiti scrawl in the sky of a cartoon: 'Are often mislabelled as hyperactive'.

The very same word that I'd been labelled with.

And there was more, because Labradors had a wow factor too.

It turned out that under all that puppyish enthusiasm they were real gentle souls. They could even carry an egg in their mouths without breaking it. That's why they were the first choice of dog when it came to caring for people.

As I read on, my mouth gaped open with wonder at these brilliant dogs. I read about a Labrador superhero called Endal, who placed an unconscious man in the recovery position without any training, got hold of his mobile phone, 'thrusting' it by his ear on the ground, then fetched a blanket, and barked at nearby houses until someone came for help. What a dog!

If they were so like me, perhaps I could yet turn out to be a human being who would actually benefit the world rather than the irksome toad everyone seemed to take me to be? How amazing would that be? I'll tell you – it would be preposterously amazing.

A huge grin spread across my face as I realized just how special these dogs were. I wanted to be just like them. Only still a person.

Later on, I discovered that a Canine Partners dog had won an award for calling help for his owner after the man had collapsed unconscious in a deserted country road. The dog had raced to the nearest populated area then made a passer-by follow him until his master was discovered and helped. I'm not even sure

I could be that smart and quick-thinking in an emergency, so how cool was it for a dog to come to the rescue?

I went to sleep still smiling that night, my mind whirling with the thought of dogs again – but this time they had more on their plate than just being my best friend.

I could almost see a Labrador dressed in a Superman costume scampering to save anyone in distress. This was important work. It started to dawn on me that this was about more than me getting a celebrity profile and a doggy chum.

But while it was exciting, it also made me nervous. All I'd really been worrying about was how to style my hair, what bagginess of jeans to go for and if my mum could wash my Metallica T-shirt in time. Now I had to up my game.

Not trying to be funny, but I couldn't help but wonder: Had I bitten off more than I could chew?

3

The big show begins, troubled teens unite

A few months later, in June, the big day had finally arrived. I'd hardly slept a wink. It was a weird feeling to wake up and feel terror and excitement at the day ahead. Usually, I opened my eyes, groaned, and buried my head under the pillow. Today, I leapt out of bed like someone had put explosives under the mattress.

'Are you up yet, Liam?' Mum shouted up the stairs, then asked if I wanted a cup of tea and some cereal.

'I'm getting ready!' I shouted back, my voice higher pitched than usual. Must be the nerves, I thought.

There was a lot to be worried about. It was like a smorgasbord of anxiety for me to feast on. I'd spent days worrying if I was up to the job, and not wanting to let my parents down. But for the moment my main fear was more immediate.

My massive ego had initially assumed this was going to be the Liam Creed show, with me getting star billing, a trailer and possibly a personal masseuse.

But Mr Blackmore soon put me right and told me there were four other unruly kids as my co-stars. I was already intimidated enough by other people, so I was silently praying that none of them would turn out to be too in-your-face. Part of me, though, knew that if the BBC had been trawling the county for teenagers with behavioural problems, it would have made sure it got ones who would make for a decent show. That meant that the kids were bound to be gobby.

The dogs I could cope with, people were a different matter.

Brushing my teeth, I shuddered to think that a minibus was hurtling towards my house at this very moment, containing a bunch of other teenagers I'd have to get along with.

Of course, first impressions count. I knew that how I behaved on this initial meeting would colour their opinion of me, an opinion that could stick like a slug for the next few months. Unfortunately, I found it really hard to control what came out of my mouth, as I'd discovered too many times with soon-not-to-be friends. So instead I focused on the only element I could control: my outfit. Plus, to make the ordeal worse, there were going to be cameras capturing my every move and word. That could be tricky, so best have something nice to look at to distract the audience's attention from any bad behaviour. Thinking about it made me worried I might throw up. The good news is that I didn't.

'You don't want to be late, they'll be here soon,' Mum said to me, as she put a cup of tea on my bedside table, and gave me a reassuring smile and a wink. She was still beaming about the whole idea. She'd always been convinced that we should all be famous.

The Metallica T-shirt was still mouldering in the wash basket, so I decided to put on my finest Nirvana T-shirt and some absolutely enormous trousers, just to prove I meant business. I stumbled down the stairs and gave Mum a goofy half-grin. I could see tears in her eyes and that proud look that made me feel a bit uneasy.

'Good luck, Liam!' Mum shouted after me as I walked into the fresh air and headed towards an experience that would change my life. Of course, I didn't know that yet.

The bus was white with a glitzy red stripe emblazoned down the side. It smelled mainly of mud, wet grass and what I have since realized is eau de dog. It has a musky quality, which starts out unpleasant, but after a while you get completely used to it and it's like it isn't there. My sister tells me that boys have a similar effect on girls.

I smiled and waved sheepishly at everyone else on the bus, as a man with a film camera waved his hand, as if to say, 'just ignore me'. I ambled to a seat at the back, making sure my fringe covered my eyes. I quickly scanned the bus to take in all the faces. So far, so normal; these kids didn't look too bad to me. I wondered what I might look like to them. I was definitely the tallest.

'Hi, Liam, nice to have you on board,' shouted the driver, briefly glancing over his shoulder before he set off. 'I'm Jason, and I'm here to help with anything you need during your time at Canine Partners.'

I nodded my head, and mumbled something back at him. Later I found out his full name was Jason Cummings and he was a youth worker whose job it was to look after us, and make sure we were coping. After all, we'd been chosen because we were prone to massive meltdowns, and not making the best of things. It might sound soft, but it was a real comfort to know that there was someone on hand to take care of us. As with most of the youth workers I've met over the years, he came across as a really cheerful, friendly guy.

Shuffling in my seat, I got my bearings and looked around at the other troubled teens sharing the bus with me. On the seat next to me was a blond boy who looked younger than me, then at the front were two girls sitting together, already giggling and getting to know each other. One had brunette hair scraped back into a ponytail and the other had mousy hair falling by her ears. Sitting alone was an unidentified object that it was pretty hard to tell whether it was a boy or a girl. Whatever it was had its hair swept so thickly over its face that it was hard to make out any features. I couldn't help staring, my mouth gaping open.

The blond kid followed the direction of my stare and mouthed a theatrical whisper to me, saying, 'Just ignore it!'

I chuckled and did a thumbs up. Why did I do a thumbs up? I don't think I'd ever done one of those as a meeting gesture. In fact, I don't think I'd ever been so friendly to someone straight away. Normally when people attempt to initiate conversation with me I just grunt and look away.

Then, in a more normal tone, he leaned across to introduce himself. 'Hi, I'm Rob,' he chirped, extending his hand for a good old-fashioned handshake.

Rob had a sweet and cheerful smiling face, round with an almost angelic chubbiness. I wondered for a second if I'd got on the wrong bus, and we were off to choir practice or something. How could this golden boy possibly be a delinquent?

I couldn't think of much to say back, so I just muttered, 'All right,' and looked out of the window in embarrassment. That's more like it.

'What's your name?' he persisted, despite my rudeness.

'Liam,' I said shyly, turning back to look at him.

He beamed broadly at me, and from that second I knew we would be friends. I can honestly say that I'd never met someone so friendly, not my age anyway. If this guy was troublesome, what the hell were they going to make of me? We were like chalk and cheese. But this whole situation was so strange that it didn't matter.

Glancing around the bus, I realized what a weird bunch we looked. The two girls looked like they'd rather be absolutely anywhere else than hurtling through the countryside in a bus with other surly misfits. They'd stopped talking and were both wearing the kind of sulky expressions that suggested they weren't jumping with joy at the idea of spending a few months tending to animals. The whisper was that the unidentifiable hairstrewn object was definitely one of us. In fact, it was even a girl. I tried making polite conversation with Rob, but during the lulls in our stilted conversation I didn't know where to look.

I hated to be in girls' company, it really put me on edge. Having spent most of my recent school life without any girls, I struggled a bit whenever they were around. That's right, old Mr Tough Guy couldn't deal with being in the presence of the opposite sex. To say I was self-conscious is the most laughable understatement of the year. Around girls, it felt like everything I did and said was so cringeworthy I might as well explode on the spot. If you haven't ever seen a man go the same colour as a pillar box, believe me, you're missing quite an amazing sight. My blushing was legendary in Chichester.

Rob obviously didn't have such problems, and confidently chattered to the girls, as well as to me. This guy was obviously at home with crowds. But as the bus got deeper into the countryside, and closer to Canine Partners, I noticed that he fell into an anxious silence. I joined him in gazing aimlessly out of the window. We'd left the town and suburbs behind and were cruising along country lanes, hemmed in by green fields scattered with sheep, cows and the occasional horse. Even though it was only a twenty-minute drive from my house, we never had time to get out into the sticks much. Not that I'd ever have wanted to if my mum had suggested it. 'Nah, boring,' would no doubt have been my reply.

But I found the empty spaces and patchwork sky of blue and grey clouds quite soothing. It was really quiet, and I smiled as I noticed a thatched cottage. It just looked so old-fashioned.

Rob didn't seem to be on the same wavelength though. The further we drove, the more agitated he became. I later discovered that his nickname was the Volcano.

I was about to find out why.

As we turned into a narrow, long, gravel driveway leading to the Canine Partners dog centre Rob suddenly flipped. It was scary to watch someone switch gears so quickly.

'I don't want to go!' he shrieked at Jason, standing up and making his way to the front of the bus. 'I want to go home! I don't want to be here!'

The outburst caught Jason by surprise, and he looked back over his shoulder in shock as he guided the bus to the side of the road and pulled over. I sat there fidgeting nervously with the cuffs of my hooded top as Rob carried on screaming and shouting.

Wow, I thought. He sure packs a lot of volume into that

little body. He was like a firebrand. His angelic, chirpy expression from before had been replaced by a look of pure rage, and an emotion I recognized well – fear. We all felt it. But Rob couldn't deal with it. It was weird watching someone else lose it, rather than me being the one having a crazy moment. Not a pretty sight. Bloody hell, they've got their work cut out here, I thought, and almost chuckled out loud. It suddenly dawned on me what a motley crew we were. I'd always been the problem kid, but now I was surrounded by them.

I couldn't decide whether to join Rob in his meltdown, or run away. To be honest, I was a bit scared. It's not nice watching someone else go to the dark side. For the very first time – after fifteen years – I felt what it must have been like to be an onlooker when I was having one of my funny turns. Were people frightened of me? I hoped they weren't, but for that split second a massive wave of sadness about myself swept over me. Just for a second, mind you.

The bus stopped and Rob was allowed out to get some air, calm himself down, and let off steam. I tried to make eye contact with him from the inside of the bus, thinking, I know that feeling all too well, buddy. It was scary, but also strangely comforting to find someone who could behave as angrily as me. I knew he'd calm down, I always do. Jason, who was trained to deal with exactly this kind of mishap, was a star. I could see him talking to Rob in a quiet, soothing tone, and after a few minutes, Rob's face started to return to normal. Goodbye, Volcano, nice Rob was back. Thank God.

He hung his head with embarrassment as he climbed back on the bus and tried to avoid looking at anyone. The two girls were biting their nails and giggling nervously.

'You okay?' I asked, sweeping my fringe out of my eyes for once, so I could look at him properly, and try to say silently, 'Don't worry, I've been there.'

'Yeah, sorry about that, mate,' he replied with a small, thankful smile. 'I lost it a bit . . .' He trailed off.

Yeah, we'd seen that. But why?

We didn't get any explanations. I understood. After all, through my zillion detentions the only thing I'd managed to tell my parents was 'Dunno'. Despite appearances, Rob was troublesome too. Not just me, then.

As we passed the last of the lush green hedges and stone walls, the road finally opened out into a car park. Well, that's probably giving it a bit too much credit. It was a small field full of grey gravel, where staff and puppy parents could park their cars. A car park by default.

So that was it, I thought. The mother ship. When Mr Blackmore had said I was going to be on telly, I'd expected something more glamorous. Film studios and such. It definitely didn't look like the kind of place where I might bump into Brad Pitt and Angelina Jolie. Nothing sparkled, and yet this was supposed to be show business. Excuse me for not jumping for joy. It looked, well, normal.

As the bus came to a halt Jason turned around to us with a stern look on his face. The cheerful man who had picked me up from home was nowhere to be seen.

'Keep your language under control, be as good as you can be,' he said, 'and, above all, just don't let yourselves down.'

With that we hurtled noisily off the bus, immediately letting ourselves down.

The gravel crunched under our heavy feet particularly loudly as we scampered up the path, like dogs finally let off the leash after a long journey, howling with joy. I'm not sure what we were so excited about, I think it was seeing more film cameras and a sound man with big furry microphones. For some reason, we saw that as a good excuse to start gurning, whooping and showing off. Of course, being typical teenagers, the thrill of being filmed lasted all of about ten minutes.

The first person we bumped into was Nina, who was waiting for us at the entrance. She looked distinctly unimpressed. The dog by her side seemed to agree, and started barking loudly, obviously scared of the loud teenagers turning the air blue with their foul mouths. I told Rob to get lost, joking, and used much more colourful language as he bumped into me, then came screeching to a halt right in front of Nina.

'Right, first off, calm down,' she shouted. 'You're already frightening the dogs!'

We all zipped it, and stood silently, shuffling ever so slightly like awkward teenagers do. There was a look in her eyes that demanded obedience. I didn't know it then, but this scary woman with eyebrows that could punch you and a tongue that could whip you afterwards was about to orchestrate an experience that would change my life.

She wore beige slacks, a green, baggy Canine Partners T-shirt and sturdy-looking black boots. Her jet-black hair was scraped off her face at the sides, but the rest flowed down her back, spattered with grey. Her eyebrows were a fierce scrawl above her eyes. She was a lady, but, my God, you could tell she had balls.

'Follow me,' she barked in her Australian accent. Or maybe that was the dog.

Either way, we trotted behind her, not wanting to risk her wrath. We saved that for later.

Nina was the first person we met from Canine Partners. She was the resident dog guru, an expert on animal behaviour, who could turn even the most unruly pup into a superdog. But she had her work cut out with us.

I scanned my surroundings, noticing concrete buildings, wooden sheds and flowerpots brimming with colour peppered about the place to give it a summery feel. It was a hot day, and the rolling fields looked appetizing away from school. For a split second I imagined all the kids at school going from class to class like a pea-green chain gang. I chuckled to myself. Losers.

Walking around, I felt like I was entering another world, one where dogs were in charge. You could see them, hear them, sense them everywhere. From the corner of my eye, I spotted a half-poodle casually calling a lift for his owner as if that were a completely normal, everyday thing to do. That wasn't proper behaviour where I come from. And yet there it was, poodle, lift, man, poodle pressing button, lift going up. Weird.

Even stranger was to come as we were led upstairs in the main building to the offices, where the all-important charity work takes place. At first it looked exactly as I'd imagined it would look – women with expensive haircuts speaking into telephones, the constant tap-tap-tap of keyboards being overworked – but then I noticed that pretty much everyone working there had a dog sitting at their feet, or slowly patrolling around their work station, perfectly obediently. It was like a strange dream. Everyone seemed really happy, and I put that down to the presence of the dogs. I'd been into a couple of offices before in my life and they hadn't felt even half as vibrant and happy as this one.

Downstairs, the building was divided into two rooms. One was a massive assembly hall for dogs, where the advanced train-ing took place. It had an air of serious concentration about it. In the other, smaller, room where the puppy parents took their scamps for their weekly lessons, a class was in progress. It was full of furry fun and boisterous yaps – basically, my kind of place. All the women had the same feathery blonde hair and happy welcoming smiles, while their perfumes disguised the heavy scent of dog. These particular puppy parents were people in the local area who looked after the pups during their first year and made sure they were happy, well-adjusted tail-waggers before they moved back to Canine Partners for training boot camp.

I wasn't an expert, but I could tell the dog centre was a converted farm. There was another large building nearby – presumably the farmer's house. Inside there was a kitchen, a big assembly hall (not quite sure what a farmer needed that for), and little offices and crannies that had probably once been bedrooms. We came to what must once have been a large barn, a place for milking cows, or rolling hay bales, or parking tractors. The whole complex had a feeling of old and new. Bits had obviously been added on the cheap. It felt like school, only friendlier.

We walked past a gaggle of dogs, prowling about in their cages like tigers (only, um, dogs), both groups examining the other with interest.

Unfortunately, then we were led back into the assembly hall and asked to sit on uncomfortable-looking white plastic chairs. Nina was not looking like a happy chappy.

So much for getting away from school, I half chuckled to myself. We were straight down to business.

'Right, hello, kids, I'm Nina and this is Canine Partners. First up, I think we should go around the group and introduce ourselves, then I can tell you a little bit about what it is that we do here.'

Her voice was stern and angry, she had her arms folded like a serious housewife, and something told me that she much preferred dogs to teenagers with behavioural problems. As I have since learned, first impressions might be important but they're not always right. She is one of the most inspiring and jovial people I have ever met.

But for that moment, it felt like she was the enemy.

Forgetting his previous eruption, our resident Volcano got up first. 'I'm Rob, and I like drama and acting,' he said in a confident voice. He was clearly used to talking in front of people. Nina looked on approvingly as he chatted about himself, coming across as a likeable little chap. But with a sheepish glance towards Jason, he also added that he could be quite aggressive. Talk about understatement.

Meanwhile I was wishing my baggy jeans could swallow me up. I was slightly (scrap that, enormously) less confident about taking centre stage, and as Rob entered his fifth minute of yammering I started to worry that my introduction of 'Liam, from Chichester, fifteen – NEXT!' might appear a little threadbare.

I needn't have worried though. Next up was Katrina – the unidentified bus creature – who was crawling up the walls with fear. She was looking at her feet, and just shook her head defiantly when asked to speak. A wallflower who had crippling shyness problems had been placed among us noisy kids with serious swearing issues. I instantly felt sorry for her, mainly because I can be pretty shy too, but manage to cover it up with some champion cursing and stomping around.

To help save her, I decided to swallow my nerves and jump in. Very gentlemanly of me, I know. I must have been overcome by the powerful dog fumes ponging the place out. I cleared my throat, hoping for a dramatic moment, but sounded like I was choking. Finally I managed to croak out: 'Shall we move on to me? I'm Liam, fifteen, Chichester!'

The shy girl looked relieved, and gave me a bashful grin. It wasn't all for her benefit either. I was relieved to have said my little piece and got it over with, so I sat there beaming.

'And why are you here, Liam?' asked Nina, alluding to the fact that we all had 'issues' of some sort to address. It was like being in detention, but more fun.

'Because I'm a cheeky little toad, miss!' I yapped.

Everyone started laughing, and the two other girls (whose names I found out were Allie and Ellie – seriously) looked very impressed. They must have liked what they saw, I told myself, knowing how wide of the mark I probably was.

'Calm down, everyone!' She nodded at me. 'It's very nice to meet you, Liam.'

'Likewise.' I smiled, giving her my best grin, the one with all my teeth showing. Actually it was probably more of a scary grimace than a nice smile, but my heart was in the right place when I did it. I hoped she realized that.

That went pretty well, I thought, surveying the hall feeling way more relaxed. I couldn't help but zone out as Allie and Ellie introduced themselves – both had bad reputations for showing off in class, just like me – starting to examine my surroundings instead. The walls were painted bright white, with instructions for the dogs – well, for the handlers to pass on to the dogs. I'm supposing that the dogs can't read. Yet. No doubt it's only a matter of time.

In fact, it felt like every one of the walls was crammed with important information and details of new techniques we were soon going to study. Everything about the place was geared towards learning; wherever you looked there was something to read, or someone ready to teach you something new. We could see Canine Partners staff milling around, and every now and again one of them would pop their head round the door to check out the new recruits. I've never had a job, but the staff all looked happy and relaxed, not stressed out like the other people I knew who worked (sorry, Mum).

Looking after dogs was clearly a doddle compared to hard graft.

'Right, that's the easy bit over, now the real work begins,' Nina announced sharply after the introductions were over with.

The dog by her side stood up as if by magic. He'd got a daft look on his face and his tongue was lolling out in the heat. His tail was swishing from side to side, and could easily have passed for a blond feather duster. I'd noticed almost at once how much the dog seemed to trust Nina. You could see the wary look in his eyes when it came to us screaming kids, but he didn't doubt Nina for a second. If she wanted him to help show us round, he would.

We were in proper, deepest countryside – it was like having a splatter of bright green explode in your eyes. It was full of rolling fields, blue skies, the kind of place where everything smelled of cow dung and no one seemed to mind. You could actually hear the nature without having to listen closely. I could hear birds chirruping in the trees, and hens squawking in the far distance. Every now and again the silence would be broken by the faraway sound of a plane flying overhead.

I breathed in deeply, and fell in line behind Rob, who

was leading the way. Already the group had started to form alliances. Rob was the unofficial leader, and I was his sullen henchman. Allie and Ellie were tight with each other, but liked to tease us lads. Only Katrina was a loner, straggling behind. It's bad news if you're the outsider with a bunch of outsiders, and I felt sorry for her.

After walking through the building, we loitered outside the entrance awkwardly, while Nina had a word with another member of staff. The initial excitement had worn off, and now reality was sinking in. This would be the centre of our world for the next three months. It was an uncomfortable thought. I could see Rob's face change, and I could tell it was getting too much for him again. 'Are you all right, mate?' I whispered to him, so the girls couldn't hear.

'I can't deal with this,' he replied through clenched teeth, his face getting redder.

Oh no. Eruption time.

Suddenly, Rob stalked off towards one of the rolling fields, muttering and swearing under his breath.

'What now?' asked Nina with an exasperated sigh, racing after him, with Jason following closely behind.

'What's wrong with him?' snorted Ellie, looking at his rapidly disappearing figure in surprise.

Nina had caught up with him and they were clearly arguing.

'He's making us look good,' I quipped, 'we should be thanking him.'

She laughed, and for a second I felt good about myself. Then I felt bad that I'd raised a laugh at the expense of my new friend. After all, I didn't have many to spare.

Out of the blue a strange and unfamiliar noise filled the air. It was the sound of tiny howls, yaps and playful growls. It wasn't a loud noise, but collectively it was like the rumble of distant thunder. But with fur on.

Another group of puppy parents had arrived.

My heart leapt, did a circuit round the car park and returned back under my over-sized T-shirt at the sight of the dogs. They were like a massive ball of happy energy hurtling right towards my life. The parents looked pretty chirpy too, laughing, greeting each other and trading funny tales about their dogs.

'He likes to eat socks,' I heard one of the parents say with a laugh, as the scamp strained at the lead to say hello to his other puppy mates. 'He even ate a pair of our Emily's knickers,' she chortled, trying to stifle her giggle with her hand. The truth was, it was no laughing matter and she knew it. Even the smallest bit of disobedience could strike him off the list for being an assistance dog. No doubt the parent hoped he'd grow out of it – after all, it was their job to straighten out these funny quirks.

Is one of those my dog? I suddenly thought. I'd been so wrapped up in the drama of meeting the other kids, I'd forgotten about my date with dog destiny.

As if she'd read my mind, Nina marched back from her ruck with Rob and said, 'Okay, now let's meet the dogs.'

Rob tagged behind her forlornly, embarrassed that he'd screamed that he wanted his mum to come and pick him up during their argument.

We might look like full-grown adults, but we were still pups ourselves really.

I couldn't believe how nervous I was about meeting my dog for the first time. Get over it, it's *only a dog*, I told myself firmly, trying to ignore my sweaty palms.

Suddenly, from the corner of my eye I saw a streak of blond fur tear through the flowerbed, and lollop across to us, with one of the staff trailing behind him.

'Liam, meet Aero,' said Nina, rolling her eyes as she introduced me to my new best friend, who had made quite an entrance.

He looked up at me with bulbous eyes, his tongue hanging heavily from his mouth, panting like he'd been thundering around the field all morning. His coat was a mess. He had a welcoming look in his deep brown eyes – the colour of chocolate

Smarties. Strangely, I felt very self-conscious as I inspected him, rocking from foot to foot with my hands in the pockets of my jeans.

'Liam, Aero, Aero, Liam,' Nina continued, with a broad grin. Seeing the dogs we were meant to train had lifted her mood after the showdown with Rob. She might not have that much faith in us, but you could tell she believed in the pups.

'Nice to meet . . .' I began, then stopped myself because I thought saying 'hello' to a dog sounded completely stupid. What would be next? Shaking his paw?

Instead I knelt down and stroked him, which seemed like a far more appropriate greeting. He looked at me, and gave me a doggy smile, as if to say, 'All right, mate.'

'Aero is your responsibility now,' Nina said firmly, as if to underline the commitment we had taken on.

I glanced up and could see the other kids waiting to meet their new doggy charges, and looking at me curiously to see how I would deal with mine. Rob had overcome his nerves and was peering over Nina's shoulder with a wide-eyed look and a smile playing on his lips.

'No probs,' I chirped, clumsily trying to tidy up his messy coat with my hand. Aero looked like he'd been dragged through a bush backwards, and his scruffy style made me feel at home with him. He didn't seem as intimidating as the intelligent, well-groomed dog sitting patiently by Nina's side.

Nina then demonstrated to us all how to put a leash on a dog, using Aero as a model. He loved being the centre of attention, and wagged his tail excitedly, doing as he was told. Nina ruffled his fur, muttered 'good boy' and fed him something she pulled out from a bum bag strapped round her waist. Aero lapped up the treat, and I could see his pink tongue slobbering over her fingers as he gobbled it down.

'Now it's your turn, Liam,' she said, handing me the leash so I could have a go at putting it on Aero.

Right. How hard could it be? But with a rash of nerves prickling up my spine, it was harder than I'd imagined.

I stood in front of Aero, awkwardly brandishing the leash like it was a heavy length of rope. I closed my eyes and took a deep breath, desperately attempting to remember Nina's brief demonstration. She had talked throughout while casually taking the dog, attaching a collar and hooking on a leash. It looked simple.

But now, standing there peering down at Aero, it suddenly didn't seem such a doddle. I played possibilities over in my head, and was disturbed to note that one of them involved me timidly approaching Aero, just seconds before he flew through the air and sank his teeth into my jugular (granted, perhaps I watch slightly too many gory films). I froze. I was frightened of an Andrex pup. This was a new low point.

By now the others had been introduced to their dogs, and after the demonstration on Aero were busily trying to get their guys on leashes too. I looked over at Rob who seemed to be a natural at this whole lark. He'd got the leash on first time, and the dog was sitting happily by his side smiling almost as much as Rob.

I hesitated, overcome by a feeling of imminent doom. It was a leash not a nuclear warning system, but right then it had pretty much the same effect.

'What are you waiting for, Liam? He won't bite you.'

I stepped forward. Aero looked up at me. Make this easy, please, I begged with my eyes. I lurched towards him, he yapped. I took a second for breath, then lurched again. Yap number two. This wasn't going as swimmingly as Nina's demo. Note to self: stop lurching. I made my approach less jerky, creeping forward, the leash held out like a man with a net trying to catch a rare species of butterfly.

'That's it, be calm and he's calm,' encouraged Nina.

I'd made it pretty far before I grabbed at the young dog's neck like a clumsy wrestler attempting a new move called the 'throat slam', unleashing a world of yaps, growls and snarls. In one enormous movement I leapt back, until I was right by the entrance to the dog pound, shaking like a leaf and stuttering with shock that I'd messed it up.

'I'm out of here,' I said to Nina, shaking my head and yammering that I never wanted to come back to Canine Partners or see a dog again. A bit melodramatic, I know, but I felt like I'd come a cropper at the very first hurdle, and it hurt my pride.

Nina smiled reassuringly at me, and gestured that I should give it another go, placing her hand gently on my arm. Somehow it did the trick and soothed me. I looked up at Aero to see if he'd managed to dial the police yet over my clumsy attack (after all, these are superdogs, I wouldn't put anything past them – even the ability to turn a little toerag like me in to the police).

Looking at Aero from a short distance away he looked calm, unbothered by the incident he'd endured a minute ago. His eager face gave me hope. Usually when I botched up something, people looked at me as if I were a piece of dirt that belonged on the sole of their shoe. Aero was different. It was like he was *willing* me to succeed.

Okay, I thought, new tactic this time. I decided to play it casual, and simply stroll over and put on the leash. As if it were the most natural thing in the world. And I promised myself that this time I wasn't going to give up. I was going to get that leash on even if it meant being on the receiving end of a bloodthirsty mauling from a sweet little Labrador. Luckily, Aero wasn't feeling particularly blood-crazed that day.

I ambled up to him, a stupid grin on my face that matched his own goofy look. Then at the last minute I fixed Aero with a serious look – he knew I meant business. No yapping, nothing, he was putty in my rather sweaty palms. It was still an embarrassing fumble, but this time I persevered with the awkwardness of trying to keep the youngster still. Through a world of doubt and a lot of sweat, I managed to get the collar round his fluffy neck and attach the leash. Within minutes, there he was, all collared up and looking superb. He looked up and gave me a congratulatory wink. Okay, he didn't. But in my mind I imagined that he had. We'd made it – we were now officially a team.

'Good boy!' said Nina, glowing with pride.

I didn't know if she was talking to me or Aero, but I lapped up the praise too just to be on the safe side.

She then threw some doggy treats on the floor for Aero to gobble up, and I have to admit I almost fancied having a nibble on one myself.

Right then and there I learned my first important lesson: positive reinforcement, not threats, work best: on people and dogs.

4

One man, well . . . boy, and his dog

I'd seen Crufts on telly before, but never really paid it a great deal of attention. From what I could tell, some well-turned-out toff would jog around, with their dog simply copying everything they did. It looked a doddle. However, a doddle it is not.

'Right, kids, now we're going to make our dogs sit without touching them or speaking to them,' chirped Nina, before demonstrating what she meant a couple of times. It was all about gesturing with her eyes, like a Jedi mind trick. And just like the perma-smiling men and women proudly prancing around at dog shows, she made it look like a doddle.

I looked down at Aero, gnawing and prodding around by my ankles. How hard could this be? I'll answer that straight away, it was completely impossible. 'Aero!' I blasted to get his attention. He looked at me, startled. I held his gaze and pointed at the ground, willing him to understand that I wanted him to sit, but he continued to stare at me, totally confused, then went back to gnawing on whatever had his interest now. I tried to keep his focus on me a few times, and getting his attention wasn't a problem. But with so many bees and flies and creepy-crawlies zipping around in the Canine Partners outdoors, he was easily distracted. Eventually I decided simply to get him sitting down by any means necessary – forget this silly hands-off, silent approach.

'Sit,' I yelped, lunging forward and pushing his lower back to make him sit. He let out a yap as I awkwardly grappled him again, morphing into a deranged wrestler, pinning him to the floor, hoping that Nina might ignore that I had taken a rather brutal route and applaud the sitting dog. Only he wasn't really sitting. This wasn't going too well. You'd think I'd have learned my lesson from the long-winded leashing debacle, but no.

'Liam, you need to be patient,' said Nina, spotting my obvious impatience.

I checked my watch; we'd been hard at it for three minutes. I made a mental note to let things happen in their own time.

'So what did you learn today?' asked Mum, sitting on the sofa as I strode in, the smell of dog wafting in with me.

'Not much,' I huffed. 'I learned that training dogs is bloody hard.'

'Well, of course it is, darling, it's probably like raising a kid, and that's no walk in the park, let me tell you. Now refill this, will you?' Mum passed me a cup.

I knew the drill, it was her relaxation time, and I made a mean cup of tea. Of course I didn't drink tea myself; giving an ADHD kid caffeine would be like giving sleeping pills to a narcoleptic, only with exactly the opposite results. For Mum I used two bags of PG Tips, a splash of milk, and half a teaspoon of sugar.

I sat patiently at the kitchen table, waiting for the kettle to boil, wondering how on earth I was going to get that dog to obey my commands without me having to sprawl all over him in frustration. I needed to find a calm, patient place, and quickly. My mind full of Aero, I rinsed the cup in the sink, and without even shifting my gaze from the kitchen window grasped the teabags and plopped them in the cup; on autopilot I reached up to the shelf and grabbed the sugar, then side-footed over to the fridge and splashed in the exact measure of milk, still thinking just about my dog. It was only as I plonked the fresh brew down on the coffee table in the lounge that it dawned on me that I'd just carried out something without even thinking about it. It was like a Eureka moment, only slightly less groundbreaking and dramatic. I hadn't reinvented the wheel, but I did realize that repetition was the key to learning. Watching Mum making her five daily teas had taught me how to make a good cuppa. I must have made hundreds, and now it was second nature. All she had needed to do was pass me her cup and I knew what was up. That's what I need to do with Aero, I thought, clicking my fingers to make it seem like it had been so obvious all along.

Mum and Dad were thrilled by my tales of single-handedly taming a wild beast who went by the name of Aero. I think it was the most conversation they'd got out of me in a year. Usually they had to make do with such descriptive insights as, 'Yeah, it was all right.'

The next day I reported to Mr Blackmore, buoyed by my success. He seemed genuinely pleased that my time at Canine Partners was already making a difference to me. What a result! Doggy treats all round!

Sadly, the same can't be said of my next trip to dog world.

Even though everyone had a serious attack of nerves on our first visit, it was only Rob who had hit the panic button. For the most part, we were all on our best behaviour. But by the next week, it all felt a bit more familiar. We were more at ease round each other and could be ourselves. Big problem. BIG problem.

Feeling relaxed enough to 'be ourselves' was not ideal for a group of teenagers with behavioural problems who were in the last chance saloon.

Of course, any group meltdowns made for good television, but we'd long forgotten about the cameras following us around. I was still geared up to be a celebrity, but we'd all started to realize that this was real, and other people's hard work and happiness were at stake. Not just our place on the next *Celebrity Big Brother*.

We were trying hard not to mess it up and let everyone down.

But we didn't try hard enough.

Basically we were a nightmare with bells on.

When we were working with the dogs, as we were most of

the time, it was fine – we'd all become silently obsessed with the idea of making a puppy sit without saying anything or touching it – but once left to our own devices, matters could get out of hand. We were, after all, disruptive kids. We did exactly what it said on the tin.

For me, I loved being around Aero, but being with the other kids was a different story. It wasn't that I didn't like them – I did – I just couldn't deal with them. As was often the case when I went into a new environment, I was nervous and edgy – hence my ADHD symptoms were heightened. I couldn't concentrate as well as people would have expected, and because I was around so many new people, I became a little bit shy and defensive.

One of my main symptoms was to pretend not to know things even when I did. I don't know why, I just found it easier to look like a dummy instead of a swot. I could tell that Nina found it annoying when she knew very well that I understood something, but instead I'd shuffle my feet, look at the floor and pretend I didn't.

If I felt uncomfortable I instantly reached for the off button.

The girls liked to make me blush and squirm (not hard!) and this only made me worse. If I knew they were watching I just folded in on myself.

On the surface, the aim of this project was for us to train dogs to help people with disabilities. But it was pretty obvious from the outset that we needed training first. I think that's how Nina saw it anyway. And I'm not sure how happy she was with the situation. I could tell that she and Jason were starting to have serious doubts about whether we could really pull this off. It probably sounded easy on paper, but now we were starting to show our true colours. We weren't so obedient and willing to listen to our teachers silently the second time around, quips started creeping in, and, I'm ashamed to admit it, so did my legendary use of language. Bad language.

So, after a good start, things were already beginning to

slide. That said, I left it until the third visit before I really combusted.

I'd been doing pretty well so far, and I could tell they'd labelled Rob as the 'problem child'. It felt good not to be the one with a question mark above their head for once. But my weak spot – girls – was about to get the better of me.

'Is that a moustache you're trying to grow, Liam?' asked Ellie over lunch.

We were sitting outside in the sunshine on wooden picnic-style benches, taking a rest from all our hard work with the dogs. To be honest, as soon as I walked away from Aero I'd felt agitated, and less in control of myself. He was like my furry bodyguard. So I instantly blushed at Ellie's comment. I wanted to be cool and laugh it off, but she'd really caught me off guard by being so personal. Normally, we just teased each other about the dogs. Having a laugh at the way I looked was way below the belt.

'No,' I replied a bit too fiercely, looking intently into my lunch like it was the most fascinating object in the world. My fringe flopped in front of my face and I hoped Ellie couldn't see how much she'd got to me. Of course, the reality was I couldn't have made it more obvious if I'd got up and done a funeral march round the buildings, sobbing wretchedly. Seeing my weakness, they went in for the kill. Bloody women.

'Are you sure? I can see some wispy blond hairs . . . Oh, look, Allie, there's a really long one!' She laughed, pointing at my sweating top lip. I was fifteen, and my hormones were involved in some sort of covert guerrilla warfare mission in my body. The latest battleground was my face, giving me tufts of bum-fluff hair to mix in with the rash of spots that usually shamed me. Teenagers aren't a pretty sight. Especially not me.

I counted to five – then lost it. Pushing my plate away in a violent gesture, I stormed away from the picnic table, swearing impressively over my shoulder as I left. I strode down to one of the fields trying to find Aero. But as I marched across the mud and grass, I realized I had absolutely no idea where I was heading, I was just walking, angrily. Normally when I was like this I'd destroy something, tear up some plants, scratch up a car. But now there was just me and open space, and nothing for me to wreck. As this thought struck me, a weird calm came over me. I huffed, strode, growled, muttered, and then relaxed. It was completely silent in the field. The sky was clear and there was nothing for me to fight against. Other than maybe a stray slug.

Calming down, I recognized the outbuilding where the dogs are kept during their 'break times'. Yes, even the animals have their equivalent of a ciggie break.

I walked past the shower area, where mucky pups were hosed down when they'd rolled in one too many fields, and went through the entrance. There was a kitchen area where the dogs' dinners were prepared and their dishes washed up. The smell of dogs was strangely comforting, and my breathing started to regulate itself. I still cringed every time I thought of what Ellie had said to me, but my anger was cooling.

The large room that housed the resident dogs was like the canine equivalent of a bed and breakfast. A path ran down the middle of the room, with around ten segregated compounds on either side. In each one of the areas, sectioned off with a metal fence, was a raised doggy bed, with green tattered blankets decorated with black paw prints (a deliberate design, not the result of the dogs getting creative with their dirty paws, *Blue Peter*-style!) There was also floor space for them to roam around when they weren't kipping or having an afternoon nap. A large metal bowl contained their water supplies, and a creamy-coloured bowl lay close at hand for lunch and dinner, always lovingly licked clean by the grateful mutts.

As soon as I walked in all the dogs stood to attention, their tails raised hopefully in the air and their eyes looking at me expectantly. A few of the dogs started to bark in excitement at seeing a human chum in their lair. Probably thought it meant food.

'Quiet, boys,' I faltered, not sure they'd listen, and worried that the others would be alerted to where I was. I couldn't face a showdown right now. But to my surprise the dogs all piped down on my command. I might have a bum-fluff 'tache, but I could get barking dogs to obey me. Barking kids might be a different matter, but I still counted it as a triumph. I wasn't fussy. A satisfied grin spread over my face.

In the furthest corner I could see a little face looking at me quizzically, his upright tail wagging so fast it was almost invisible. I strode towards him, then stood face to furry face with him. Suddenly, I felt a bit stupid. How exactly was a dog going to help me? He could hardly put a consoling paw on my shoulder. We looked at each other anxiously for a second, and then Aero broke the silence with a good-natured yap. At that, I climbed over the small fence to sit inside the compound with him. An illegal manoeuvre, I know, but at that point I really didn't care if I got into trouble or not. I sat down on the cold concrete floor next to Aero and softly stroked him, more to soothe myself than anything. Weirdly, I felt more at home in the doghouse than at school, and the shame of losing the plot in front of everyone started to fade.

Funnily enough, Aero didn't have anything that useful to say on the matter. But I didn't mind, I wasn't about to hold it against him. He nuzzled into my hand with a few almost silent woofs, and I began to feel a bit ashamed of my overreaction.

'So you're here then.'

I looked up and saw Nina in the doorway. Her voice was stern, but her eyes were warm. I think she was touched that I'd turned to the dogs in my hour of need, rather than tried to get the hell out of there, like Rob.

'You ready to come back?' she said, holding out a leash towards me.

I looked at my watch. It was time to get Aero ready for our next training session. 'Yeah, I'm ready,' I replied, reaching out for the leash, but looking down. I appreciated her coming to find me, but I still felt stupid for flying off the handle at the girls' teasing. I was a typical teenage scumbag, terrified of anything in a skirt.

I paced behind her as we walked back towards the hall, Aero gambolling behind me, sniffing random nothings in the air and giving short yaps at passing birds and butterflies. It was hard to stay upset for long here. I even felt oddly happy.

Aero raced ahead into the hall, pulling on his leash, obviously wanting to be the first one to face the girls again. He was braver than me. Rob fell in step with me, asking if I was all right, as his dog sniffed Aero's bum. Dogs, eh? No manners.

'Ignore 'em,' he said wisely about my two female tormentors. 'There's too much other stuff going on to let them get to you.'

'Yeah, I know,' I replied, looking into his pale blue eyes. I appreciated his pep talk. first because I knew *he* knew how it felt. He was the Volcano, after all. But it was nice to have a proper mate for once, backing me up. I realized just how lonely I felt at school. You try to toughen up, but it's hard when it's just you against everyone else. I was surprised how good it felt to have someone on my side, someone looking out for me.

'You're a good mate,' I blurted out in the heat of the moment.

Rob looked stunned then grinned, saying, 'Cheers, Liam. Have you ever seen *Billy Elliot?*' he added, almost shyly, as an afterthought.

I shook my head. I wasn't big on films, unless they were the big action blockbusters. 'Why? What's it about?' I asked curiously, tickling Aero under the chin to keep him happy as I chatted to Rob.

'It's a film about this kid from up north who wants to be a ballet dancer. But he's a lad, so everyone takes the mickey out of him and he has a hard time . . .'

'Oh,' I replied, not knowing where Rob was going with this. I didn't really know much about ballet. Wasn't it some guys prancing around in white tights?

'I want to be a dancer,' said Rob quickly, taking a deep breath as if it had been a big effort to spit it out. 'Like in musicals and everything,' he added.

I shrugged my shoulders. It did seem a bit weird. I'd never met a bloke before who wanted to be a dancer. Some of Sophie's mates went to dance classes, and wore funny-coloured shiny leotards, though I'd never really paid it much attention. But it didn't bother me *what* Rob wanted to do. He could have wanted to be a pantomime horse for all I cared. Along with Aero, he was one of my first real friends. Sad but true.

'Cool,' I offered up as a response. I couldn't really get into a deep one about pirouettes or anything, but I wanted him to know it didn't matter to me.

'Yeah, I think it's cool. But not everyone at school does . . .' He trailed off, and I could fill in the blanks. I was just the kind of gobby idiot who might have had a field day with that kind of information back at school. It's a bully's dream, isn't it?

It explained a lot. Rob seemed a genuinely nice lad, he didn't find it hard to express himself like I did, and you could tell that everyone liked him; he always had a right old natter with Nina, and he was a natural with the dogs. But then he could turn nasty. Before this chat, his transformation into the Volcano hadn't made much sense to me. But now the pieces were starting to fall into place. I could see how he would have a really hard time at school, and how it could mess him up.

It was a bit of a novelty to put myself in someone else's shoes for once. Like I've said, the problem with ADHD is you get trapped in your own dramas and tend not to relate to other people, or what's going on around you. If people have a sympathy gene, it seemed like mine had been on a very long holiday. But maybe it was back in the country because I looked at my new friend and rather than feeling sorry for myself after Ellie's nasty dig at me, instead I found myself thinking more about Rob and feeling sorry for him, and what he was having to deal with.

All round, it seemed like I was about to get a crash course in empathy.

73

Aero stood by my side, and it sounds silly, but I felt like he was proud of my new-found caring side. Bonkers, I know.

As Rob and I took up our training positions with the dogs, I slid into a wheelchair without giving it a second thought. I'll repeat that: I got into a wheelchair.

The hall was full of props to train the dogs, and, thinking about it, it must have been a weird sight. But there was so much going on (mainly in my tiny little brain) that I hardly paid it any notice. Because the dogs would eventually have disabled owners it was important that we understood their limitations when we trained the dogs. So the hall had a couple of wheelchairs for our use, and we sat in them without giving a second thought to what it really meant to use a wheelchair. It's shameful to say, but, like pups, at that stage it still felt like a game for us. So we zoomed around in wheelchairs, with the dogs by our sides, without taking on board the implications of what it might be like if we couldn't stand up and walk away from those chairs.

Another prop we had to use was what I like to call a 'ticker': it was a little device we used to let the dog know that it had done something well, or was at least going along the right lines. It had a little button on it that made a snappy clicking sound, and it was fairly small – probably no bigger than a bouncy ball – so if Aero was setting about one of our challenges in the correct way, I'd press the button to let him know he was on the right track. In human terms it'd be like telling someone they were getting warmer or getting colder if they were looking for a hidden object. The idea with this was that the dog would come to associate the noise with success, and, eventually, that overcoming obstacles would lead to tasty treats. The treats were reserved for when a challenge had been met, while the tickers were there to encourage the dog to keep going. It's an ingenious idea really, and thus I was rarely without my trusty ticker in my pocket, ready to offer Aero little clicks and clacks of encouragement.

I'd noticed that lots of the doors around the Canine Partners' building had dangling rope attachments on the handles, and at the end of the rope – probably about a foot long – was a tennis ball. I'd thought they were curious door adornments, but before I'd found a moment to ask what they were all about, I'd been distracted. There was much in this place to capture the imagination. It would have been a bit like asking Willy Wonka about the paintwork in his chocolate factory.

'Some of you might have been wondering why the doors have rope on them,' said Nina.

I felt like shouting out, 'Yes! Yes, I had been wondering!' But instead I played it like I'd never even noticed, letting out a weird inquisitive sigh instead.

'Well, they're there so that the dogs can open the doors.'

Of course, it seemed so obvious when she pointed it out. I'd heard that one of the skills we were going to teach these pups was how to open a door, but I'd assumed it would jump up and use its nose, or grab a doorknob in its mouth and twist. But no, this made much more sense.

The idea was that the dog would take the tennis ball in its mouth, pull the rope and the door would open. Easy.

'Grab the rope, Aero!' I demanded, pointing at the door.

Aero wandered over to the door in question, then looked over his shoulder at me. What next? I gave him a treat for making it to the door, where the rope dangled limply in front of his nose. He sniffed it.

'Grab it!' I enthused, pointing repeatedly at it, like an old woman on holiday trying to buy a cake in a foreign language.

Aero was looking at me eagerly, desperate to know what the hell I was on about, but with little in the way of an idea. That was the great thing about my dog in those early days – he really wanted to help me out, but he just couldn't always understand what I wanted. He was keen to please and full of energy.

Suddenly, in one motion, he grabbed the tennis ball, opened the door and wandered nonchalantly through it. I damn near squealed with delight. He looked at me for approval. I gave him a treat, a cool, calm pat and he returned the compliment by licking one entire side of my face.

Also in that massive hall there were actual life-size washing machines, so the dogs could learn how to open the door, then load the washing and take the clothes back out.

The first time I saw a dog do it I just cracked up laughing. The golden retriever lifted his big paw on to the handle at the side of the door and pushed hard until the catch unlocked, then dragged the clothes out of a basket with his mouth, and finally pushed the door closed with his nose, then looked up expectantly at the trainer.

'How did he do that?' I asked Nina with a mixture of laughter, bewilderment and admiration. 'That was awesome!'

Nina explained that they used treats to teach them. A dog would sniff around the machine, and as soon as their nose touched the bit that opened the door, they'd get a treat. After a bit of aimless sniffing around they'd twig on to the fact that when they pushed a certain part with their nose or paw, they'd get a goodie. Labradors and golden retrievers, the two main breeds at Canine Partners, like to learn. Unlike me, they loved to figure things out for themselves and get into the good books of whoever was teaching them.

Except Aero. Nope, my stupid dog took more after his owner – well, caretaker.

Today was all about the washing machine, and Aero was having none of it. He walked round, had a sniff, and then came back to sit at my feet.

Nina could see we were having difficulty and came straight over. 'What's the problem, Liam?' she asked, her lips pursed and one hand on her hip.

'He won't do it,' I said in a slightly stroppy tone. 'He was fine with the door because it was obvious, but this is too much – I can't teach this.' I could see Rob's dog pawing the washing-machine door open, and I huffed in annoyance.

'Open the door!' I commanded Aero, my voice more raised than I intended. I was turning into one of my own teachers – agh. Aero looked at me and refused to budge. He could be a stubborn little git, but I knew I was losing my rag with him.

'Be calm,' Nina coached me. 'He can sense your anxiety and he doesn't know what he's done wrong. So he's just sitting there, not taking any chances.'

I took a deep breath, and had another go – this time trying to sound friendlier.

'Get the laundry, Aero, get the laundry.' I nodded to the washing machine again. And, suddenly, he darted towards the washer. My heart bounced, as a feeling of total joy mixed with relief completely overwhelmed me. And to think I had been seconds away from doing my usual shrug and going home disappointed.

'You see, Liam, it was only a matter of time.' Nina beamed. 'Good for you!'

Aero didn't sort the whites from the coloureds, the cottons from the silks, he didn't even acknowledge the basket next to the machine, instead choosing to drag the washing out and flump it on to the floor. But, for sheer relief, just watching him wrestle the clothes into his mouth and out of the machine was about as good a feeling as I have ever known. This was honestly the most successful moment of my life so far.

'Good boy!' I whooped, dropping a handful of doggy treats on to the floor to congratulate him and he scoffed them with his usual vigour.

With the rush of achievement still pumping around our veins, we moved on to a lesson on doggy hygiene. This was a guide as to how to keep the dogs shiny and clean, day after day. That meant hoisting Aero on to a table in front of the group and poking and prodding him, and checking his teeth, which involved pulling up his mouth to peer at his gnashers. I was grateful for his impressively patient nature.

Unlike Aero, I could be enormously impatient with him in

those early days, often sitting awkwardly in the wheelchair, staring down, convinced that he had no idea what I was trying to make him do. Even though I was probably the weak link in this relationship, sometimes I'd lose faith in him coming through for me. After all, look at him, he's a dog, I would think. He doesn't have the foggiest what I'm on about – I'm just some stupid teenager making noises at him.

After lunch we were set to meet the puppy parents – the people who had looked after our dogs for the first year of their furry lives. I was excited about meeting Aero's surrogate mummy – a lady called Susan – and finding out more about his puppyhood. He could be a little tyke now, so I knew it could have been a million times worse if she hadn't whipped him into shape.

The puppy parents are a really big deal, and they do exactly what the title suggests – they play mum or dad to the infant pups. They're probably the most essential cog in the whole machine. If Canine Partners was a football team, the puppy parents are the holding midfielders making everything tick. Their job was to take the pups at eight weeks old and teach them to be cheerful, obedient and gentle.

Aero is a Labrador retriever. For those who don't know an awful lot about dogs, they're basically the best ones around (I promised Aero I'd say that!)

But seriously, that's not actually a million miles away from the truth. Following on from my research, meeting our dogs had proved to me that they really were the perfect assistance dogs, having the right balance of gentle obedience and cheerful energy. In dog circles they're notoriously sociable.

Back in the olden days, as far as I can make out, someone thought it would be a fantastic idea to breed a dog specifically geared to work with human beings and ended up with the Labrador retriever. The word on the street is that they're prone to mischief, but still the easiest dogs to train. As matters stood, I wasn't a hundred per cent convinced by the second bit. Yet.

I felt a bit shy as I was introduced to Susan, a no-nonsense-looking woman, holding a big mug of tea.

'Nice to meet you!' She beamed.

I tried to think of something nice to say back, but my mind was full of driftwood as per usual.

Luckily, at that moment Aero scampered in to say hello, looking like he'd just been stage diving at a heavy metal gig.

'So you haven't changed then.' She smiled, bending down to ruffle his already mussed fur and say hello.

Thanks, Aero, I thought. At least someone knows how to break the ice.

Labradors come in three main colours – yellow, chocolate and black. Aero was yellow, or 'blond' in human terms. Aero's coat always looked rumpled, no matter how much care and attention I put into making it look smooth and shiny and healthy.

'Did he look this messy with you?' I asked, looking quite unkempt myself.

'He's just one of those dogs.' She laughed. 'Aero can manage to get all scruffy for no apparent reason, a bit like a mischievous child,' she said with a smile, looking at me a little bit too knowingly. But Mum would share that knowing look, no doubt.

I'd already spent the night before pleading again for us to get a dog like Aero at home. Saying goodbye to him, and going back to my lonely bedroom with just Smokey's snoring for company was horrible.

I explained that Labradors were the dogs you see on adverts, flying through the air acrobatically catching Frisbees, the kind of dogs that could sense that clumsy children had tumbled into disused wells and could save them. I'll admit it, I was building them up. They were named Labrador retrievers after the region where they are thought to originate and because they're hunter/gatherers and could probably provide for the entire family, I continued.

'But we've got your father, darling,' said Mum with a chuckle, 'we don't need another hunter/gatherer in the house.'

Since starting at Canine Partners, I did understand why Mum had always said no so firmly. Dogs are a huge commitment. Aero was brilliant, but some days I felt completely worn out, and couldn't wait to get away from him at the end of the day; it took a while to get used to a creature with what seemed like a limitless supply of energy all the time. Probably a bit like a kid with ADHD, I expect.

Limitless energy wasn't all we had in common either. Like me, Aero had been brought up in a clean, happy household. Dogs need a decent home life just like we do, because, like humans, dogs can pick up bad vibes, and can be victims of their childhood. That's why making sure the puppy parents were the right people for the job was so important. You couldn't just walk in off the street and demand a puppy to train; you had to have the right mix of kindness and patience – unbelievable patience – to do the job.

As we sat on plastic white chairs, Susan sipped from her mug of tea and explained a bit about herself, and how she'd raised Aero. She told me that she'd looked after numerous Canine Partners pups before Aero turned up at her door. She dazzled me with lots of interesting facts, and once again I was surprised to come across a grown-up who wasn't just decent, but actually quite entertaining.

Above and beyond anything else, dogs require a lot of maintenance. It doesn't matter how much you train these cheerful animals, they're never going to clean their own teeth, or get in front of the mirror to check their coat is neat and tidy. All this grooming is done by the people looking after them; silly as it sounds, I hadn't really thought of any of that. Poodles don't do their own hair, big sheepdogs aren't whiter than white because they washed their coats themselves. A person did it. When Aero had a wash, so did I.

I'd always seen dogs as big smiley beasts to run around parks with. But I suppose to a lot of people they're like kids and looking after them is a really serious business. Already, still early in my time at Canine Partners, I was starting to feel a little bit protective of Aero – in a brotherly rather than fatherly way, I should point out. I'm too young to be a dad, even by modern standards.

It's easy to forget that dogs don't understand language in the same way as we do because we're so used to seeing them around, and watching them obeying orders; but they do that because they have been trained repetitively to be obedient. They learn things parrot fashion, rather than through explanation. It sounds obvious, but it's something even I had forgotten.

By the time Aero arrived at my feet, looking for all the world like the cheekiest little angel, he only made such a great first impression because Susan had done a terrific job of training him. And, forget that I was now meant to teach him to load washing machines and mooch around supermarkets, my task was nothing compared to hers.

Labradors always want to do the right thing. But like so many humans – particularly fifteen-year-old ones suffering from ADHD – they can have trouble keeping to it. They might dig up flowerbeds when no one is looking, or chew a nice leather shoe into a soggy mush, but that's because they're dogs, and they don't know any better. The puppy parent's job is to prevent bad behaviour through the early days, as well as deal with the inevitable downsides of looking after a pup that is new to the world. I am, of course, referring to house-training, which can seem to take for ever, until suddenly they get the message and know that they have to go outside to do their business. Until then you have to be prepared to clean up after them without scolding the puppy. Labradors, however, are one of the easiest breeds to train in this respect.

When Aero first went to Susan's, he would have been a frightened and confused small pup. After all, he would have been recently separated from his mum and the rest of his litter. Hence, like babies, he would have cried and whined during the night, but the trick when training puppies is to ignore their screams. It sounds hard, and it really must be. But unlike tiny humans, dogs need to learn to be alone, and the only way little Aero would have learned that night-time is for quiet and for sleeping was by example.

Another big problem with young pups is that they don't know their own strength. Even their tiny puppy teeth can be pretty painful, and like naughty little gnashers, they often play by gnawing away on your hand or foot. Anything. The puppy parent has to stop that kind of crazy behaviour. The pups need to have their boundaries set and put into place.

One way to do this is to make sure that they constantly get enough exercise. Puppies have boundless energy, so to distract them from mischief, the puppy parents need to find other amusements to occupy them. Namely tearing around a field . . .

Because, let's say it together: PUPPIES HAVE ADHD TOO!

The relationship with a dog will always require a lot of work, just like human relationships do; after all, who wants to hang around with people who are mean and make them feel bad? Puppies like to be around cheerful people.

The idea is to have fun, and to ignore the bad behaviour. If you don't react to misbehaviour, soon the dog will realize that being naughty doesn't get treats. What's the point in that?

Play is hugely important. If someone looks all anxious and timid around the dog, the bond won't grow. I learned quite early on with Aero that if I launched myself into play, he reacted in a far more cheerful and obedient way.

Labradors are sociable animals, they need company, and they need activities to occupy their minds and muscles. As I mentioned earlier, these dogs have been bred for training, and they're pretty clever. They just need to be pointed in the right direction.

The key is to remain positive at all times, and never get cross with the dogs – they don't understand anger in the same way as we do. In the animal kingdom, aggression breeds aggression. The dog has to learn to trust you, so your behaviour around them must be consistent, so that they get used to it. But, above and beyond anything else, your behaviour towards the dog must be positive. Positive parenting is the way forward. Well, it's the only way.

After our chat, it was time for Susan to head off for home. As I waved goodbye to her, Aero waving his paw by my side (he wasn't, but I'm sure he wanted to), I vowed to be a better big brother to him.

I was going to be the best damn trainer in the world of doggy rearing – handsome, calm and always in control. Well, maybe not quite so chiselled of jaw, but definitely not too hard on the eye.

I owed it to Aero – and myself.

5

A celebrity visit, and a big breakthrough

With dogs on the brain, my next challenge was a total surprise – because for once it didn't involve anything that had four legs and woofed.

As our bus drove through the countryside morning sun towards Canine Partners, I gazed out of the window and daydreamed about myself as a champion dog handler, complete with a strange patterned waistcoat and a sequined shirt – don't ask me why, that's just the image that came to mind. I pictured Aero with the wind blowing through his fur in a movie-star manner, running in slow motion, and myself with gleaming teeth and a hairstyle that resembled a blow dry. I couldn't wait to see Aero again, I was practically champing at the bit.

But as we walked into the hall there was a distinct dog-shaped hole. Not a yap to be heard. 'What's going on?' I whispered to Rob.

'Okay everyone, something different today,' said Nina with an enigmatic smile. 'I'd like you to meet someone . . .' As her words trailed off, an athletic-looking man, with huge shoulders and a friendly smile, wheeled himself into view.

'I recognize him off the telly,' I said excitedly to Rob, prodding him in the side.

Every so often when I was at school details from a subject we were being taught would stick in my mind. It didn't happen often, I grant you, but from time to time something would slip through the barriers and stay with me. It might be an expression, or a turn of phrase, or a cool name. It could be anything.

For instance, I'd enjoyed the story of Captain Scott that we'd been told about in history one afternoon. I liked that he had spirit, even though he'd essentially failed to do what he set out to achieve. For those who don't remember, he's the guy who raced some bloke to the South Pole, but came second and then died. I admired him for being a terrier, doing his utmost to prove people wrong. I wanted to find a bit of that spirit in me – although, of course, my intention was to do it without dying in the process.

Another item that stuck with me was a line or expression about not judging someone until you have walked a mile in their shoes. It might have been from the Bible or somewhere. I'm not sure. It felt appropriate now that I was at Canine Partners. And, in a way, it was starting to make sense why they had chosen to take wayward children on to this course instead of normal, everyday high-flyers. We knew what it was like to feel different, we were society's young outcasts, and yet, in many ways we were open to other people. It might sound odd, but I think I was less judgemental than most. I was often just happy for someone to talk to me – even if it didn't really show sometimes.

The point being, we were probably more comfortable than we realized about meeting and getting to know disabled people. They had physical problems, we had serious behavioural ones.

'Say hello to Ade, a champion basketball player in the UK,' said Nina proudly.

I'd seen him on a BBC programme, and I instantly felt a bit starstruck – I'd never met a proper celebrity before. Ade Adepitan had been a star of some of those little clips they had between shows on BBC One too. He had dreadlocks which looked really cool, and the friendliest smile I'd seen, probably ever. But, if I'm being honest, I also felt a bit awkward because, yes, he was in a wheelchair, and he was far trendier than me. On both counts, I felt like I didn't really know how to talk to him. My illness is such that occasionally I can blurt out the wrong thing, and I was worried that I might insult him somehow.

It's only since my time at Canine Partners that I've realized that it's damn near impossible to offend somebody in a wheelchair by making a reference to it. They are, believe it or not, completely aware of the fact that they're moving around with an aid that most of us lucky ones have little use for. Plus, they're used to people, notably kids, staring at them. Such behaviour isn't meant to offend them, it's often just innocent curiosity. It took me a long time to learn that I shouldn't be fearful of disability. It's just a fact of life for some people.

Anyway, in the case of Ade, I really needn't have worried. He shook my hand enthusiastically and gave me a broad grin. He was so cheerful and open it felt easy to fall into a casual banter with him. The fact he was in a wheelchair didn't seem like a problem for him, for us, for anyone. But, in reality, of course it was, and we were about to find out why.

'Hi, everyone,' Ade addressed the group. 'Today we're going to find out what it's *really* like to be in a wheelchair, and some of the difficulties disabled people face on a daily basis. The plan is for us to head off to a local supermarket, and see how you all cope doing your shopping in a wheelchair.'

A collective murmur broke out at this news. We'd all used wheelchairs in the confines of Canine Partners, but this was something else – it felt pretty scary.

For this exercise we were going to play the part of a disabled person, as opposed to the part of the dog trainer, the idea being that we needed truly to understand what it was like to depend on one of the dogs. We had to get some kind of perspective on how important the course was. We were still prone to acting up from time to time and not taking the training as seriously as we should. We were improving, but we were far from perfect.

Sometimes, what with all the drama of training our dogs, it was easy to forget what we were training them *for*. And, we were pretty wrapped up in our own problems too, so it was hard to imagine what other people might be going through. This would be a big learning curve for us – and we needed it.

When we first arrived at the supermarket there was an uneasy silence. Luckily Ade didn't stop cracking jokes, and this really helped us feel more comfortable.

As usual I treated the whole exercise like it was a laugh, partly this was because Ade was so lighthearted, but also because that was the way I dealt with anything difficult. Zipping up and down the aisles was fun. I was surprisingly nifty in a wheelchair, having spent much of our lunch breaks up until now attempting to learn how to do wheelies – which I knew full well Ade could do, having seen him with my own eyes.

Unfortunately, while the zooming about was like second nature to me, it wasn't long before I'd gone hurtling headlong into a sticky patch. I wanted a tin of hot dog sausages from the top shelf, and suddenly it didn't feel so funny that I couldn't just step out of the chair and reach up to get them. I looked around dumbly, wondering what I should do. I've always found having to ask people for help particularly difficult. One of my ADHD symptoms is to bottle things up. But I couldn't just avoid this. I'd got a shopping list, and part of the task was to buy everything on it. I really didn't want to fail and let Ade down. So I loitered around the freezers awkwardly umming and ahhing for about fifteen minutes until I plucked up the courage to ask a passing elderly gent for help. It felt strange, a young lad like me asking an old codger to help him out, and I realized that this was what Ade – who was really fit and capable – must feel like. All the chat about 'giving disabled people more independence' started to make sense. I could see how important Aero would be to someone who was disabled. This was about way more than just the two of us training each other for the hell of it.

It was as much an exercise in pride, and even, in my case, swallowing it. It might sound terrible, but I'd often felt sorry for people in wheelchairs in a pitying way, a condescending way. Yet, in the short morning spent with Ade, I understood that they, for the most part, don't warrant our pity at all. He was far more capable than anyone I'd ever met of coping with whatever life threw at him; that was obvious from his confidence. Our dogs were simply being trained to give people who deserved their independence some freedom. I knew now how important that was. I'd walked a mile in someone else's shoes and it had really opened my eyes.

With the sausages safely in my shopping basket, I headed for the checkout, feeling a mixture of elation and sadness as it dawned on me what it meant to be disabled.

'Altogether that's nine pounds and thirty-two pence,' said the girl behind the till, leaning forward out of her chair and smiling down at me.

I rummaged around in my pocket for the ten-pound note that Nina had kindly donated, and handed it up to her, careful not to move too far forward, just in case I went arse over tit.

As I left the supermarket, head held high, I felt a bursting sense of pride and achievement.

Nina was outside, beaming that enormous smile of hers in my direction.

'Well done, Liam!' She clapped. 'So how was it?'

'Honestly?' I said. 'It was totally petrifying, but after a while I think I just about got the hang of it . . . not easy though.'

'It opens your eyes, doesn't it?' she said, nodding knowingly as she spoke.

Definitely.

With an important lesson well learned it was time to say goodbye to Ade.

'Kids, I really hope you can now see how important what you're doing is,' he said, as we all listened, nodding enthusiastically.

Unless I was entirely mistaken, it looked like a couple of the girls might have developed a bit of a crush on our kindly basketball star. They seemed totally awe-struck. Ade had had quite an effect on the womenfolk. Something I'd hope to aspire to myself one day. I made a mental note to start smiling at people more. It was a good look.

After thanking Ade for his help, we headed back out into the countryside. When we arrived, my next task should have been a doddle – especially compared to what we had just done. But this was the weird thing. Sometimes it was the smallest jobs that got to you. Like washing my messy dog.

Nothing filled me with more dread than washing Aero. Oh, it was a nightmare! Just awful. I could stroll into the shower area with every intention of keeping myself dry, but anyone who has ever seen a dog emerge from water knows that's completely impossible. They shake themselves around in a drying frenzy, like they're doing some kind of weird apocalyptic jitterbug, spraying water absolutely everywhere. Or, in this case, all over me, my amazing hair, my clothes, everything. He might leave the shower area with sopping paws and a pristine coat, but I'd traipse out in serious need of the world's most efficient and boiling-hot radiator to dry my drenched clothes. Or one of those incredible Dyson hand driers that appear to be cropping up all over the place. Only I'd need one for an entire human being. After about three or four watery encounters I twigged that it might be worthwhile taking along a change of clothes. Not the sharpest sandwich in the picnic, I know.

This afternoon, as the water gushed powerfully, I scrubbed Aero vigorously to make sure that his coat would stay fresh and clean for as long as possible. My logic being that the better turned out I could make him, the less time I'd have to spend in the future tending to his every hygienic whim. That was, of course, all a massive waste of time. Dogs will always manage to become unthinkably filthy given half a chance. With so much mud and nature to bomb around in, keeping Aero nice, sparkly and minty fresh was one of the most futile exercises I have ever embarked on. And I once started a 1,000-piece jigsaw – which I didn't finish.

Meeting Ade that morning had really touched me, and I was in a thoughtful mood. I think Aero could sense it, as for once he wasn't his usual scampering, playful self. Instead, he stood there all doe-eyed, looking up at me as I directed the hose on him.

My thoughts turned to how much I could feel myself changing as a person, and what a big part Aero played in this. Others in the crew – like Ade, Nina and Rob – had a big impact, but it was this young dog who was really making the difference. Because we had been thrown together, learning lessons at breakneck speed, it was sometimes hard to keep up with our developing relationship. We were definitely on a journey together, one that was exciting and new to us both. Yet, even so, when we were left alone to do what we liked I could sometimes get a little bit shy. Let me repeat that: I would get a little bit shy . . . in front of a dog. Weird, I know.

I wasn't used to being alone with people, unless they were doctors or members of my family. Whenever I'd played with other kids I'd noticed how their parents would loiter around, I assumed to keep a close eye on me, what with my appalling reputation. No one really trusted me to be left to my own devices, but so far at Canine Partners there had been many times when it appeared that I was coming dangerously close to being treated like an adult. It was both enthralling and daunting at the same time.

So when Nina wasn't there to tell us what to do, neither one of us really knew who was boss. I was becoming increasingly aware that I was there to learn something about myself as well as teach my dog to be the best-trained Canine Partners puppy around. Without an authoritative voice yapping at me, I became more and more conscious that I was the adult in this relationship. That was a role I wasn't used to. Even at home with a younger sibling I had always been the child in most need of instruction.

After his wash, I walked Aero out into the yard. We had some free time, and as Aero looked up at me, it was hard to suss out what he wanted to do. He just stood staring at me, not breaking his focus, even with a cloud of crows flying overhead squawking loudly.

'What is it, boy?' I said, genuinely desperate to know what to do next. 'Do you want a walk?'

He didn't break the gaze. I hooked on his leash, and decided that a walk was what we needed. By the way he walked next to me, then in front of me, and then dragged me by quite some distance, it was exactly what he needed after all. It might sound like a small deal, but it gave me a big confidence boost to know that I could make the right call. I didn't need Nina standing, looking over my shoulder, telling me what I should be doing next.

Afterwards, we headed back to the hall to continue with our training exercises. Following on from the morning, our task was to lead the dogs around a pretend supermarket, getting them to help out where they could.

But even though I was growing up in so many ways, and learning stuff about myself, and the world, my confidence was still a problem. Thanks to my ADHD, I was used to my inability to concentrate – I'd always had that – but the awkwardness of becoming a teenager had hit me pretty hard. The worst part was my crazy blushing. And when I say 'blush', don't underestimate where I'm going with this. I don't mean that my cheeks slightly flushed for a split second, I mean that absolutely every drop of blood in my entire body would surge into my face, which would light up like a big neon red light saying, 'Look at me and laugh,' made all the worse if I started sweating too. If that happened, it was unlikely to stop. People, of course, found it funny.

The blushing was a signal of my lack of confidence, which everyone at Canine Partners picked up on, especially the youth worker on hand to talk to us and check that we were coping okay. He could spot that underneath all the bravado, I was probably just an unsure and timid kid trying to find his way.

'How are you coping with the others?' Jason would ask.

There was a time when I was reluctant to speak openly to youth workers, and viewed them as much the same as teachers. The enemy. But, over time, I'd come to realize that they were there to fight our cause; it was their job to help us, to locate the decent human being lurking beneath the grotty façade. I'd thought Jason was a good bloke right from the start; he didn't talk down to us, and he appeared genuinely to care about how we were getting on. I was happy to tell him how it was.

'I'm doing okay,' I said. 'I still haven't settled in properly, I'm struggling to relax when we're in groups, but I really like Aero, he seems . . . sound.'

'Sound' was probably quite a strange way to describe a dog, but that's what he was like, how he came across. All round, a sound little pup.

'I still get frustrated though,' I would admit, reluctantly.

Often with Aero I would get in a total huff if I didn't know the answer, or said the wrong thing during training. Nina patiently explained that it was completely all right to say the wrong thing from time to time, and it didn't matter that I didn't have all the answers. It sounds obvious now, but it came as a blessed relief to hear that I could make mistakes without feeling completely stupid. Unfortunately, even though my triumphs with Aero were building my confidence, this fragile scrap of self-esteem fell apart as soon as girls were in the picture.

With just five of us kids on the programme, there was a real hothouse atmosphere – and the fact that over half (well, three of the group) were girls made that difficult for me. Katrina kept herself to herself, skulking around with her hair hiding her face, only really bonding with her dog. At break times and meals she sat slightly apart from us, only joining in with the odd comment or snigger. Ellie and Allie were a different matter, and together they were pure, giggling, schoolgirl trouble. I liked them, but I *dreaded* them too, if you know what I mean. They brought out all my worst aggressive, defensive, show-off traits. I suppose in a primitive way I wanted to impress them. Sad, eh? But I couldn't help myself. I was a teenage boy to the bone.

After the showdown over my bum-fluff moustache, things went downhill. The two girls knew they'd hit my weak spot, and from then on it was like one of those wildlife programmes when the predators go in for the kill.

I was feeling a bit emotionally wobbly after our morning with Ade, and crisis point hit during the afternoon break. Ellie had another verbal jab at my moustache, and I lost it. She'd been systematically mocking my facial hair from the start of the course, slowly breaking me down like she was using water torture. So I was growing a small moustache? Who cares? I couldn't work out why she found it such a source of amusement.

In the first week, I had found Ellie overbearing and hard to take, but as the days wore on I realized that underneath it all she was actually quite sweet and funny – her teasing me wasn't malicious. I wasn't even usually that bothered by her comments, but I was having a bad afternoon. I'd been all fired up to take on the world and turn Aero into a superdog, but it hadn't gone quite according to plan. Aero was having an off day, and had been staring at me blankly while I was taking him around the pretend supermarket for the umpteenth time; if it were the real world, some poor bloke in a wheelchair would have to spend the next week living off one tin of spaghetti hoops and some kitchen foil! I may be a teenager, but even I know that none of that makes for a balanced diet. After my experience in a real supermarket in the morning, I had seen how important this all was. But, unfortunately, I was almost about to blow it.

Maybe it was all too much for me. My ADHD meltdown switch flipped on, and my frustrations boiled over into the kind of nasty outburst which often got me excluded from school.

'You growing a tache?' Ellie mocked for the gazillionth time, looking over at Allie, who then also broke out into a cruel chortle.

'At least I can shave my moustache,' I growled back. 'Pity you can't get rid of your acne!'

'Get lost, Liam, shut up!' shrieked Ellie, biting her bottom lip.

'Why? You going to cry? Oh, poor little baby,' I mocked, like a right little oik.

Whoops. Remember, I live in a house with two women.

I'm not stupid. I know that if you attack their skin, or skincare regime, it's like a declaration of war. It's about as low as you can go. Ellie had got a problem with her skin, and you could tell she was self-conscious about it. I couldn't help going for the low blow.

I knew straight away that I'd said the wrong thing. The entire table was walloped in the ears with the kind of silence that is so quiet that it's almost noisy. Then the seconds tick-tocked by in slow motion like they do when you're waiting for a toddler who's just fallen over to break out into a crescendo of hysterical weeping.

On cue, the tears flooded from Ellie's eyes, her face scrunched up into a painful expression, and she started sobbing. Meanwhile, like a superhero in reverse, I'd morphed into the worst human being on the planet. I was Bad Man.

Rather than saying sorry, I arranged my face into a surly smirk in the most obnoxious manner ever. I'm just glad Aero wasn't there to witness my horribleness. He might have thought twice about his new friend.

What made the whole drama even worse was that as she ran off in tears, Nina was heading in the opposite direction, towards our picnic table. She deciphered exactly what was going on through the hyperventilating and sobbing as Ellie dashed off. A shadow of disappointment crossed her face as she looked at me.

I leaned back on my chair, still smirking. I think the expression was welded on by then thanks to a mixture of shock and embarrassment. Deep down I really did feel bad, but I couldn't show that or explain it to anyone. On the surface I must have seemed smug.

Tragically, this was how my smooth conduct around women operated. Just so you know, I'd like to explain right now that I'm not proud of what I said, not remotely proud of it. Quite the contrary. I'm ashamed of how I behaved, but how can I possibly write the true story of myself and Aero without giving an accurate description of how mean I could be? The journey towards being worthwhile is as much about me as it is about my dog.

Sure enough, as soon as Ellie started crying, a massive pang of guilt (the kind that I always get when I've been mean) hit me in the chest area. Allie set off in pursuit of Ellie, growling over her shoulder, telling me where to go. I was behaving at my worst, picking on people for no real reason, hot and bothered, just because I was frustrated. I like to call it 'ADHD Liam', the one who gets muddled and wound up, and whose brain starts blitzing from one direction to the other. It's probably a weird feeling when the hazy mist descends, but I'm used to it now.

Rob – another lad with a magnificent temper – looked on, shocked and startled by my enormously unimpressive display. I could feel my face hitting tomato-alert, my lip somewhat quivering, searching for a quip. I was out of line. I knew that.

'Mate, bit harsh.' He shook his head in despair. 'You certainly know how to hit a girl where it hurts.'

His disapproval made my cheeks burn even more with shame. By now, Rob and I were solid mates, and I knew that if he thought I'd been bad, I really had been bad. I'd got carried away, like I always do, and taken things about a million miles too far.

'I've just about had enough of this, Liam.' Nina sighed.

I sat there in my usual deflated pose that I save for when someone is telling me off.

'Every time I think I'm making some progress with you, something like this happens. You tell me, what am I supposed to do?'

'I don't know,' I harrumphed. Once again, the adults are turning against me, I grumped to myself silently, and, yes, stupidly.

Unfortunately, and totally predictably for a 'problem child', I'd developed a bit of an issue with authority. This was mainly the result of the hours wasted sitting in detention, or in the headmaster's office, feeling hard done by or bitter. Even if I knew that a teacher was secretly trying to help me, like Mr Blackmore always was, I still didn't want to lose face.

My mind formed a rude response to Nina, like one I might have spat out at school, but the words wouldn't come out.

Canine Partners was different to school in so many ways, and I couldn't be my usual offensive self. There was a nice straightforwardness about the place that I wasn't used to. The instructions were simple: teach these dogs to do good things, and good things will happen to you in return – namely, you'll feel a glowing sense of achievement. And beyond that, your dog will change the life of a disabled person. I have since learned that this process can be called altruism – benefitting from helping someone else is the gist of it.

As Nina stared expectantly at me, I remembered the beaming sense of pride I had when I did something right, and how much better it felt than bodging everything up.

But we were all still wriggling around, desperately trying to break free of the shackles that came as our baggage. Namely the various aggressive or shy defence mechanisms that we had come to rely on, the phobias, the isms, the ADHDs.

Having been selected for this project because we had bad reputations or behavioural issues, for the first stage there was an element of keeping up with our reputations. We were all from different schools, so there was a silly (in hindsight) desire to prove that our school was the toughest. My argument was that because there were no girls at my school, it was bound to be much tougher, so I had to protect my street cred by being systematically aggressive. Just remembering that makes me feel embarrassed. Such a waste of time.

This was the ridiculous attitude that I'd taken to school with me every day for years, but the difference here was that I loved waking up in the morning and heading out to play with Aero, and seeing what tricks we could come up with that day.

I wanted to fall to the floor and beg Nina for her forgiveness,

I wanted to tell her that I wasn't that horrible surly adolescent any more and that I was so sorry for what I'd said to Ellie. I really was. I was even a bit embarrassed – it's not nice making girls cry. Especially as I really like girls – or, at least, the idea of them. But, instead, I sat there in total silence, my face fixed in a grump. The stubborn side of my nature was totally unwilling to let her see just what a great time I was starting to have.

'You've been showing great promise. Aero seems to like you, and you seem really to like him.'

That made me smile – on the inside, of course (show no weakness).

'But I'm at the end of my tether. You kids have got to take this seriously, it's not a joke; these dogs don't understand the situation, so if you're not behaving appropriately, it could affect their training.'

I rolled my eyes, stupidly. Big mistake.

'Liam, more of this kind of behaviour and you'll be off the project, and back to school full-time. You need to realize how important this is,' Nina said, with a pause for dramatic effect.

My heart went thud, right about to the bottom of my stomach. One thing I certainly didn't want was to be dismissed and sent back to school, especially as everyone probably expected me to fail at this too. Already I'd been at the dog centre longer than anyone expected.

She looked me in the eye, almost like a challenge. 'I know you can do this,' she asserted, still holding my gaze.

And before I could puff out my chest and crack some clever remark, the tears spilled from my eyes, and the bottom lip went into random jerking mode. Ah, rats.

'I'm sorry,' I spluttered, 'I do really want to be here, don't send me away.'

Nina handed me a leash. 'He's waiting for you.'

'I'm sorry, Ellie,' I said, shame-faced. 'I honestly didn't mean it.'

'That's okay.' She smiled, the rims of her eyes still burning red. 'Apology accepted.' Both of us had calmed down now and returned to the fold.

I walked towards Aero, who was sitting in the kennel area waiting for me. I knelt down and he trotted over to say 'hi'.

'Sorry I'm late, buddy,' I said. 'I had a few behavioural issues for a change.'

He smiled at me, and from what I could gather he nodded at the leash. It was his way of suggesting we go for a jog around the field, get a bit of exercise and banish all the negative energy.

Thus far, 'walkies' weren't entirely as I'd imagined. I'd seen a million people walking dogs in the past and they always looked totally in control of the process. Either I was wrong, or they had been taking extra PE classes on the side. It's the dogs doing all the walking and the humans are getting dragged along. The fact was that Aero pulled me around that field at Canine Partners, him a puppy, me half running to keep from having my arm pulled from its socket. It was probably a sign that Aero was in charge. Out of the two of us, my behaviour was still the worst.

The day had started out hot and sunny, but as I looked up into the sky I noticed a band of heavy, grey clouds coming in from the west. Technically I didn't have to take Aero for a walk, as we'd had a trot round the field earlier, and maybe it wasn't such a good idea to get caught out in the rain – especially as I'd already washed him. But Aero looked up hopefully, and I knew he was right. A walk was the only way to clear the buzzing in my head after my flare-up with Ellie.

We'd only got as far as the yard when Nina appeared in front of us.

'Forgotten something?' she asked with a knowing smile.

I'd already apologized to Ellie, so I couldn't work out what she meant. I looked suitably bemused, and Aero and I stood, both staring at her quizzically.

From behind her back she produced something in her hand.

I started to laugh, and Nina cracked up too. I was forgiven – but not off the hook.

My mind flashed back to the first time Nina had presented me with this item – and my look of total horror. My jaw dropped so far I must have looked ridiculous.

'And what is this?' I'd snorted, with my head cocked sideways, hoping I was wrong about my suspicions.

'What do you think it is, Liam?' Nina had smirked, a little too sadistically for my liking. She'd looked like she was enjoying it all a bit too much.

I'd looked down at the object in her hand, and noted to myself that it looked like an innocuous plastic bag. But I knew, deep down, that this wasn't just any plastic bag.

'I think I know,' I'd sighed with a disgusted resignation.

'I think you know too.' Nina had chuckled loudly. 'Would you like to check with me, see if you're right?'

'Is it for dog poo?' I'd asked, scrunching up my nose and virtually spitting out the words.

'Yes it is, Liam,' she'd replied with comic triumph.

Oh, fantastic. I was right in the doggy-do as you might say. On that first occasion Nina had struggled to make me understand why I needed to clean up after Aero. My first reaction had been, 'Ew – no way!' It had sounded like a disgusting joke to me.

Now though, I reached out my hand and took the plastic bag without so much as a murmur. I didn't mind clearing up after Aero. After all, it was the least I could do for the little fella. He depended on me, and I was happy to be there for him. That was a big first for me; the difficult kid, who had leaned on everyone else, was happy to be there for someone else.

When I told Mum I'd had to scoop Aero's poop, first she'd fallen about laughing, then she'd given me a big hug and said, 'It's your wow factor.'

Come again? Dog poo is my wow factor? What a recommendation. Not.

But she'd explained how I had been happy to change my sister Sophie's nappies when I was younger. She took it as a sign of the caring side of my personality. There was a nice Liam busting to get out, she said. A Liam with a nose of iron, it seemed. But nice?

After my little outburst with Ellie I wasn't so sure.

But at least now I could see where I was going wrong.

My training was working too. Even I couldn't understand why I was becoming so damn sweet.

6

Impossible things become possible, like good behaviour

By now, going to school was even more of a chore. After six weeks on the programme I had found somewhere I'd much rather be than a stuffy classroom with snotty teachers. Yet my history as a troublemaker had all but been erased. Cleverly, my teachers knew exactly how to keep me quiet. If I so much as squeaked out of line in class they'd threaten to pull me out of the course. It was a devious move on their part, but it sure worked as a deterrent. My behaviour improved noticeably, and I was virtually walking around polishing my halo like a perfect student. More than all that, though, I was learning from my own teachings.

Much like my pup, I was a creature of habit, so weaning myself off mischief was harder than you'd expect. In class I was notorious for my wisecracks during lessons, the ones that often found me beckoned to the front of the room to sit under the watchful eye of whichever teacher I'd offended. Now, I wouldn't say I exactly took pride in my cheeky outbursts, but they were a fundamental part of my personality. In fact, scrap that, I was often proud of them – I was convinced that my cheek and wit were what made me who I was. Without the jokes, I'd be like Superman without the whole being-able-to-fly routine. Dull.

It was an important lesson to learn, but I came to recognize that perhaps dull isn't such a bad thing. After all, people who toe the line never seem unhappy, and they certainly don't have their free time dictated by punishments.

'Oi, Liam, fancy a smoke at break time?' asked one of my unmentionable classmates.

'Yeah,' I said, in a knee-jerk reaction. I then did some basic maths in my head: smoking + getting caught = trouble. I didn't fancy trouble. 'Actually, you know what . . . um . . . no, I'm all right.'

He stopped in his tracks. 'You sure about that?' He looked into my eyes, as if to check whether it was the real Liam Creed in there.

'Yeah, I'm sure . . . I, erm . . . don't fancy it.'

'Fair enough,' he said, stepping away slowly, looking at me with suspicion in his eyes.

I felt a weight lift from my shoulders. Saying no was liberating. It became a bit of a habit, and it wasn't long before I was declining offers of mischief left, right and centre. Mum has always said that it's hip to be square – perhaps she's right.

I'd noted that whenever Aero behaved, I liked him more, and I'd find myself feeling far more forgiving of his weaknesses and mistakes; it made me understand why the teachers hadn't liked me so much. I'd been a little bit of a prat. So I started presenting myself as a nicer guy. I began to keep my head down, and I smiled a lot. It created a positive, cheerful façade.

So I shouldn't really have been surprised when Mr Blackmore called me to his office one day. It was the second decent conversation we had experienced in there. The first, of course, was when he told me all about that strange-sounding place where they teach dogs to help disabled people by answering phones and other such magic.

'Liam, sit down,' he began, signalling for me to take a seat.

I plopped myself down calmly. I think I was probably even smiling. Or not grimacing, which was the equivalent of a full-wattage beam for me.

'I'm noticing a huge improvement, we all are,' he said, sitting on the corner of the table facing me. 'We're all proud of this turnaround.'

I grinned gormlessly, not knowing what to say other than, yeah, I know, I'm brilliant.

'I knew you had it in you, Liam, and I'm so pleased you proved me right. You're a real success story and an inspiration . . .' Mr Blackmore went on in this vein for quite a while as I blushed deeper. But, for once, in a good way.

Walking out of his office with my head held high I felt like I was breakdancing on air.

I knew what he was doing too – I'd learned the very same technique at Canine Partners. He was using 'positive reinforcement', congratulating my good behaviour, so that I would feel further inclined to be a model citizen in the future. It worked, it felt great, and although I spent every waking hour counting down the hours until I could be back with my dog, it felt liberating not to be in trouble all the time. The teachers spoke to me, and even looked at me, completely differently.

People talk about living for the weekend, putting their heads down and forcing their way through the boring weekdays. But I just assume that those people haven't found an interest they're passionate about. For me, I had two weekends every week, the one where I had the day off school and headed out to learn more about my intriguing new pal, Aero, and the actual weekend that everyone else got. It wasn't long before those were spent swotting up on dog training too. It's funny looking back, because no one, not even me, would ever have thought that I'd find something I wanted to do for ever, because I'd never seemed particularly keen on doing anything at all – but suddenly I'd not only found an activity I was all right at, I'd found my ideal job. How many kids in their teens could say that? Not many, I expect. Without wanting to sound too overdramatic, it was like I'd inadvertently stumbled across my whole reason for living. Okay, that probably does sound totally dramatic. But I mean it.

I'd never sought approval before. In fact, quite the opposite: I'd always gone out of my way to be disagreeable, and wanted disapproval. I'd always cheered on the bad guy in films. Beneath the sneers and costumes, I'd assumed they were just misunderstood, like me. That isn't to say I'm some kind of evil devil child, just that I've always been drawn to controversial characters. One of my favourite singers of all time is Marilyn Manson – that pretty much sums it up.

Plus, I've been told that teenagers who come from relatively quiet surroundings are further drawn to introspection – we don't have a high street to keep up with on a daily basis. Kind of makes sense, I suppose. But the point is that I wanted everyone at Canine Partners to like me – that had literally never happened before. And the reason I wanted them to like me so much was because I really liked them. There wasn't a single person working there who didn't go about their day with a smile on their face. Just going through those gates and up the drive would fill me with optimism. I was dangerously close to being happy. Actually cheerful. Being used to school, I hadn't yet experienced a big group of people getting on so well.

Even the dogs seemed on a high.

After making such a gigantic mess of everything at school, it was like being handed a clean slate. The only hurdle I had was that part of the playground had joined me on my journey of self-discovery: the other kids, the four other members of the Famous Five. We were all there for different reasons, and as the weeks rolled on it became more and more apparent that some of us were in greater need of it than others. That's not to say that I was enjoying a fresh start that was completely wasted on the others; rather that they probably didn't need it in the same way as I did. Rob, for example, had already found his purpose – as Billy Elliot with anger issues. Canine Partners was having a positive effect on him too, but, unlike me, I think he was happy when the day came to an end and we all climbed back into that white minibus to be driven home. The four of them would seem cheerier on the way back, while I was more animated on the way in.

'You're becoming a bit of a geek, Creed!' they would tease with good humour.

'Bollocks!' I would guffaw back, pretending that I was still the same old Liam who turned up on day one.

But if my new mates at Canine Partners poked fun at my dedication to dogs, the kids at school were starting to wonder if my big TV story had just been a yarn – dog guru and minor celebrity? Where was he? It had been a while since all my talk of celebrity, and none of us realized that it took ages to get to the screen, through numerous editing suites and cutting room floors.

As I walked along the corridor, still on a high from Mr Blackmore's verbal equivalent of a doggy treat, I heard a booming voice behind me.

'Oi, Creed! When are you going to be on telly? We're still waiting.'

I turned around slowly. I knew that voice. It was a burly kid, Mark, in the year above – *not* a friend of mine. I winced, wishing Aero were with me to go in for the kill (okay, so maybe he'd just lick him to death). I winced as I noticed that Mark was about ten yards behind me, and he'd brought an army, roughly four men strong. Well, exactly four men strong, all a year older than me.

'What? Um, soon, it takes a while . . . long process . . .' I muttered, wafting the thought away, and speeding up ever so slightly. I didn't want them to catch the scent that I was scared.

'Slow down, Liam,' he shouted, sprinting until he'd caught up with me.

I stopped, turned around and closed my eyes, ready for whatever cruel trick they had up their sleeves. Were they going to mock me? Or would this involve more than words? As far as I could remember, I had no beef with Mark. I wasn't particularly fond of him, but neither our paths nor swords had particularly crossed. Until now.

'It's a documentary for the BBC,' I stuttered. 'These things don't just go straight on to telly, they're not live.'

'That's wicked, mate,' he chirped, patting me on the back as he and his army strode by and headed to the park – to play five-a-side, I expect.

I let out an absolutely enormous sigh of relief.

So the word spread like wildfire that I hadn't been making it all up. Suddenly I wasn't just the lanky bloke with the long hair who seemed always to be in trouble, I was a little bit of a celebrity. This was before I'd even been on their screens! I have to admit that I loved the attention, who wouldn't?

Even the local girls' school caught wind of the arrival of a local superstar in their midst. It was brilliant.

Of course, being a television superstar wasn't as easy as it sounded. In the early stages, knowing that we were being filmed made me really shy and self-conscious. I didn't want to look stupid on camera. But then, after a short while, any symptoms of shyness went hurtling out of the window, and instead we acted up. The cameras became part of the scenery and we genuinely forgot that they were there. I'd always wondered why people behaved so badly on *Big Brother*, and the answer suddenly became clear – they forget. They completely forget that everything they're doing is being broadcast to the nation.

As a result, it wasn't long before my going to Canine Partners became less about a TV show and more about Aero. I'd lie in bed unable to sleep because I was so excited about the next day and what might happen. It was a feeling that I'd never experienced before – normally I'd lie staring at the ceiling wondering what trouble awaited me with the morning sun. School felt like a prison, but Canine Partners made me feel free, and my senses were buzzing. Yet to the naked eye I still looked and sounded like moody old Liam, grumping around whispering profanities to himself. What no one realized was that inside I was smiling like a maniac and doing cheerful somersaults.

If I had any vestige left of my assumption that the cred of being on telly was the biggest and best thing about Canine Partners, that was about to change.

Two outings happened in quick succession that had a profound effect on me.

First up was something that sounded incredibly simple.

'The dogs have to have regular check-ups at the vet's,' Nina informed me. 'Aero is due a visit – and you'll have to take him.'

Gulp. It was like going to the doctor's – but for dogs.

So here I was, in my best (well, least faded) T-shirt, with Aero looking nervously around, sniffing at all the strange smells, then looking back up at me for reassurance. I felt his pain, really I did.

I'd been in places like this a million times. The walls were stunningly white, the smell was one of medicine and illness – a bit turgid, a hint of antiseptic, the usual magazines and comics, the same cheerful woman nattering on the phone at reception. How can they talk so much? Where do they find the time to gather up the gossip? It's amazing.

So there I sat, feeling the nervous tension, watching the parents gnawing their knuckles and trying to be brave. And yet for once, I wasn't the patient waiting to go in to be prodded and talked about. I was the anxious parent. Or in my case, big brother.

'Is this going to take long?' I asked the receptionist in my best, grown-up voice.

'If you take a seat, it shouldn't be too long.' She smiled, not realizing how hard that would be for me, with my kind of fidgeting. Because of course, it probably goes without saying, I have trouble waiting. Queues were not designed with ADHD sufferers in mind – my knee tends to start motoring, then my eyes dart around the room, and if things get really bad I might start muttering to myself. It's normal restlessness times about ten, basically.

But I was the grown-up here, so I played the part of a calm young adult, and obediently took my dog over to the comfiest-looking spot just by the window, where the sun was shining in. It seemed like a good place for Aero to have a little doze. I looked out of the window and I could see kids bouncing along the street in groups, lapping up the warm sunshine. I felt sad for a second, and a bit jealous, because I'd love to skip down the road with my pals – problem is, I don't really have any. Except Aero, of course, but he was flat out on the carpet. And probably Rob, but it was still early days there. Plenty of time to fall out.

I was making the most of a comfortable brown sofa, and pretending to read *Heat* magazine as my dog curled up at my feet. Whoever reads *Heat* will be disgusted to know that a woman who was in *EastEnders* has cellulite all around her bum.

'Mr Creed?'

What's Dad doing here? I thought. And then I realized that she was talking to me. I was 'Mr Creed'. It was going to take me a while to get used to this whole becoming-a-grown-up stuff. I much preferred 'Liam'. Although 'sir' has quite a nice ring to it as well.

'Yes,' I said, standing up, chuffed. Actually, it sounded good, I decided – I felt important for once.

'The vet will see you now.'

I gave Aero a pat, and off we popped. Him to get a quick check-up, me to feel like an adult for once. Mr Creed indeed.

The check-up was fairly basic stuff: the man in the coat had a look at his teeth, his eyes, then asked me how he was behaving, and if he ever scratched himself. Did he tend to whine? Did he ever run out of energy? It felt brilliant being asked so many questions that I actually knew the answers to. And, as I suspected, Aero was totally fine, in full shipshape working order. Just a little bit scruffy. It was funny seeing Aero with people of authority: his behaviour changed, just like mine did. We were playful and mischievous together, but in that room, surrounded by adults with furrowed brows going about their important business, we both morphed into polite young gentlemen. Aero was obedient and silent; I looked on with a fixed, serious expression. We caught each other's eye at one point. I winked at Aero, and I could tell that he was chuckling inside about this strange alien experience we were going through together. It sounds silly, but I think I could read him pretty well by then, not in a psychic way, but I could read his face.

When I got home that evening, all I could do was babble about how amazing our trip to the vet had been. I'd realized what it must have been like for Mum all those years, dragging me through doctors' waiting rooms, but never hearing very good news at the end of it all.

'You're obsessed with that dog!' Mum laughed, ruffling my hair affectionately. She had a point, and I noted that she had started ruffling my hair a lot these days. Where did she get that move from?

It was funny, whereas I used to hate talking about my day, now all I wanted to do was tell my family about Aero's latest exploits, or something amusing Nina might have said. For a grown-up, I must admit that Nina was proving to be a world of giggling and jokes – if I wasn't completely mistaken, I'd have thought that she was one of us kids. She was growing on me, and in a really good way. I think it would be fair to say that in many ways she was becoming a friend – my first grown-up friend. Had anyone told me I would think of an adult as a friend, I'd have had them tested for total insanity. But those were the facts, and what had started out as a social chore was now quickly becoming the focal point of my life. No, I couldn't believe it either.

Initially, going to Canine Partners was a brilliant reason to avoid school for a day, but the more I went there, the more familiar I became with my surroundings and the more comfortable I became with the people around me, the more I fantasized about being there in my free time. It took about three or four weeks before it dawned on me that I hadn't blushed for a while. That was incredible. I could even walk into a room with actual real-life girls in it, and I wouldn't instantly feel a burning desire to sprint from the room, and when I spoke it wasn't always total and utter gibberish. Sometimes now I made sense. Admittedly, not all the time, but still, this was progress, baby! Progress!

Above and beyond everything else, my new-found confidence meant I wasn't afraid to speak my mind, but more than that I wasn't completely terrified of saying the wrong thing and looking stupid any more. I was even, very occasionally, willing to laugh it off if I did something stupid. Let's not bound ahead of ourselves though. I was still a little oik at times, but when it came to spending time with my dog, I was the one calling the shots, and the power was going to my head. Hopefully in a good way.

On my next visit to Canine Partners, there was more exciting news.

Of the five of us who started out, by the midway point I think the one most seriously affected by the whole experience was me. That's not to take anything away from any of the other kids – we all had our story to tell – but there's a big difference between going somewhere to find out how to behave in a disciplined fashion and learning how to love yourself and have confidence. I was getting to know and like myself – not just bonding with a dog. Of the others, I'd say that Katrina was on a big journey too. She'd been so depressed that she'd taken herself away from school and other people, so just being out of the house was a big deal for her. We both had a lot of work to do, and I'm sure her story is an interesting one too. But, unashamedly, as far as I was concerned, it was all about me. Not the TV show necessarily, but the journey.

A big part in my development was watching how Nina dealt with people. She was so kind and generous, but when she was serious she still managed to get things done in a calm, pleasant way. She never seemed to raise her voice when she got frustrated and angry. Believe you me, with five of the nation's most irritating little so-and-sos to deal with once a week that was tantamount to a miracle. I always assumed that come the end of the day she probably wandered into the middle of a deserted wasteland and hurled rocks at the moon while screaming at the top of her lungs, but apparently I was wrong. She does nothing of the sort. Nina was inspiring without knowing it, and, along with Aero, she made me want to become a nicer person.

Of course, many of my problems still stemmed from my condition, and unfortunately you can't just decide away ADHD. But with the right daily dose of medication, and a bit of concentration, I knew I could grow further into being the man I wanted to become. Much of it was about trying not to react to my usual urges, to find an inner strength that gave me self-control. I found being with Aero, going through routines like washing, or playing fetch, or training, were good methods of calming me down. I could focus my mind on my pup and forget about everything going on around us. Two things made it easier for me to relax, the first being that I had only one job to do at Canine Partners – to train a dog – and the other was that I cared about it.

At school I was continually distracted, or had to endure lessons that I didn't understand, but at the dog centre, in the great outdoors, there was more routine and repetition for me to get to grips with. It was constant, the people were kind and friendly, the dogs adorable. I wasn't afraid to be there, like I sometimes was at school. There was a sense of freedom that was completely at odds with the prison-like qualities of school, by which I don't mean just my school specifically, but all schools. I needed practical training, and that's exactly what I was getting. And strangely, for someone usually so drawn to the wrong side of the tracks, there didn't seem any point in getting into trouble. In fact, after a while, I couldn't really figure out how I could get into trouble at Canine Partners even if I really wanted to. Everyone was so nice. It was fun.

'I'm not joking, Liam, it's like having a totally different son!'

Mum said with a laugh one Sunday afternoon when we'd all gone for a family stroll.

I knew she was right, but thought I might as well milk it a bit. After all, I do love to be the centre of attention. 'Ah, come off it, I haven't changed that much!' I scoffed, as we strode past little stone walls, past other families walking their dogs, past troubled teens hunched over walls chugging away on roll-ups. I would sporadically stop to stroke a dog and ask some clever question that I already knew the answer to.

'Labrador retriever, right?'

'Yeah.'

'Great dogs. They make terrific guide dogs, you know?' I would smile, strutting away feeling good about myself.

'You just seem calmer, Liam, more mature. I'm proud of you.' Mum looked at me with tears welling in her eyes. She's an emotional woman, but I could see that this was a really big deal for her.

In the same way that it was an enormous weight off her shoulders all those years ago when I was diagnosed with ADHD to find out that I wasn't just a brat, I was ill, now I could read what she was thinking: she was relieved that I could find something that made me happy and inspired me enough to get out of bed in the morning already cheerful. I knew that's what she was thinking because I was thinking exactly the same thing. All of a sudden the future was a lot brighter than any of us would have expected it to be. Before this miracle came along I was hurtling towards failure at school, then probably would clutter up various dole queues around the country – and that was us being positive and optimistic. But this showed that I could achieve something practical. I just needed to find the right path. We didn't dwell on it, but there were Creed-shaped sighs of relief echoing around Chichester. It felt good.

At the same time I felt a bit sad about the past too. It was a strange feeling, like my eyes had been peeled open, and I could now see what an irritating little swine I must have been for the last umpteen years.

'I know I've been a bit of a nightmare, Mum. I'm going to try my best to be, you know, a bit better . . . and that,' I stammered eloquently, grabbing her hand and giving it a squeeze.

I wondered what the ghost of old Liam, hunched over the wall, chugging on a badly made roll-up, would have made of the new hard-working version that I'd turned into. He'd have been impressed, I like to think, if not a little taken aback. But more than anything else, what really stuck with me was that my sudden turnaround was so damn bittersweet. It made me happy, optimistic and driven. Yet equally, on the downside, it made me so cross with myself for all the years I had wasted languishing in a vicious cycle of stroppy behaviour, frustration and all those hours of detention. The wasted time really started to grate on my mind. I could have been learning more about dogs, I could have been a good student. I don't want to blame everything on the ADHD, because from what I could tell I wasn't the only kid knocking around who had been dealt a rough hand. People all over the country have to contend with the same problems as I do. And by now I'd seen enough people struggling in wheelchairs to realize that there are people out there with problems far more debilitating and harsh than mine. I just can't concentrate some of the time (okay, pretty much all of the time).

I don't know if any of this played a part in Nina's decision. But as I stood in the hall, looking for all the world like an eager young pup, Nina pulled Rob and me to one side and uttered the few words that would change my whole view of this puppy-training business.

'Rob and Liam, you two will be heading off to London to visit a woman called Eileen, who has one of our dogs,' said Nina.

I looked at Rob; he was beaming, big thumbs up at the ready. This was brilliant news, a day out, and in the Big Smoke, no less. This would never happen at school. Again, I wanted to bound into class and declare to my old school colleagues (not really pals) that something good, yet another, was happening to me. The treats had kept on coming. That's right, folks, old Mr Troubled Teen is off to London. Big bad London. However, I knew that would be totally immature, so instead I kept it to myself, while jumping up and down inside, squealing like a demented maniac who'd just won the National Lottery.

'Eileen was thirty-two years old when she was diagnosed with Stiffman's Syndrome, which basically means that all her muscles went totally stiff, and for the next twenty years she could barely move,' said Nina. 'Now she lives on her own with one of our dogs, called Sailor. She's a lovely cheerful lady, so you will enjoy it.'

'We're going to London!' I cheered as we left the building. We tried a high five, but it all went horribly wrong, both grazing the side of our palms. Rubbish.

To be honest, when I first heard that I was to be sent off to London, I didn't realize quite what an effect Eileen was going to have on me. I was obviously more thrilled about seeing London than I was about meeting Eileen.

The journey was exciting. I'd been a couple of times with Mum and Dad in the past, and it's like going to another planet. Much as I love Chichester, it's hardly the most exciting place in the world, but London always looks so bustling and energizing. Were it not for my love of the great outdoors, I'd probably consider living there some day. Everything is bigger, brighter, louder, funnier and angrier. As cities go, it looks like it was designed by people with ADHD for people with ADHD.

Rob and I sat staring out of the window for most of the journey, only occasionally breaking away to exchange jokes or ask for another bag of Hula Hoops – I'd snaffled a few packs from the kitchen cupboard, while Mum explained in detail who I should and shouldn't talk to. It felt good to get away for the day – yet another example of my fast journey towards becoming a grown-up. I thought of all the other kids at school. This idea of appearing on a TV show was really starting to pay off, I thought.

Once off the train at London Bridge, we were surrounded by mayhem – this was nothing like the station at Chichester. In Chichester you'd be lucky to spot an empty plastic bag wafting in the breeze down the platform edge, let alone an actual human being. Here, everyone was darting around wearing serious expressions. Rob and I looked like a pair of Paddington Bears stuck in the eye of the storm as everyone whizzed past us to get to wherever they needed to be in such a hurry. Thank God the film crew was with us to keep us from getting totally lost. They knew their way around, so swept us through the station, and down to the Underground.

We took the tube to Shepherd's Bush and we kept laughing at how quiet it was in the carriage. No one spoke. They were all sitting in rows opposite one another, but in complete silence. My mind was insisting that I shouldn't laugh, but that made it absolutely impossible. I kept cracking up, it was infectious. Rob made it even worse when he started pulling faces at me.

Eventually, my belly aching from giggling far too much, we reached our destination, Eileen Hobson's house.

It was in a quiet street off a big bustling main road packed with restaurants, butchers, supermarkets, video shops, everything you could imagine. It was exactly as I pictured living in London to be; there was even a big market under a railway bridge selling all kinds of stuff, from hats and jackets, to washing powder, make-up, fruit and veg. It was vibrant and colourful. Like in the train station earlier that day, everyone looked like they knew exactly where they were going, and they needed to get there fast. I liked it, I have a strong sense of urgency too, believe it or not.

In 2005 Eileen was assigned one of the dogs trained at Canine Partners, a Labrador retriever called Sailor. This, Nina had said, was a chance for Rob and me to go out there into the real world and see exactly what we were working towards with these dogs; before Sailor, Eileen had spent years living in a hospital. Since Ade and the supermarket, we hadn't had much contact with disabled people, so this was another chance to get a first-hand insight into what we were doing. Meeting Ade in those early days had made me emotional, determined to do this right, so I was kind of prepared to be moved by Eileen, although I didn't know to what extent.

As we trundled up to her front door and pressed the door-bell, I felt those old butterflies flapping around in my stomach. It sounds silly, but I was totally nervous of meeting someone with a disability away from the sanctuary of Canine Partners. At least there we had people like Nina to break the ice and make sure that there weren't any unbearable awkward silences. For instance, with Ade she'd done a nice introductory bit before letting us kids get our claws in, and fumble around for things to say. But here, between Rob and myself, I wasn't confident that we had the necessary conversational skills to last ten min-utes let alone a whole day with someone in a wheelchair. Rob was prone to silent moods when he was feeling tired, and I was worried that I might say or do the wrong thing, as I so often do when I'm nervous or uncomfortable. Of course, as with so many lessons I've learned in life, I needn't have worried.

Sailor started barking, and I heard a woman's voice.

'Okay, boy, for God's sake, it's just the doorbell.'

I tucked myself behind Rob so that he'd be the first face they saw, and my hair spilled over my face. We probably looked like the least appealing pair of teenagers ever to pay anyone an educational visit. Then Eileen answered the door mid-chuckle, beaming a smile so bright and cheerful that it actually lit up an already bright day. I liked her instantly, and found myself hanging on her every word for the next Lord knows how many hours.

'Come on, guys, let's go and sit in the garden, it's too sunny a day to stay cooped up indoors.'

I followed her through the house – a bungalow – and was surprised by how normal it was. I have no idea what I was expecting, but I'd envisaged there would be all sorts of indications that the person living there was wheelchair-bound. But no, it looked a bit like my home, in that it wasn't unusual. My family could have lived here, were it not so tidy. Wooden floors, various shelves and cabinets, pictures from when Eileen was younger and able-bodied. She looked active in them – she'd been in the army. The smile was still the same, and over the course of the day I would take furtive glances at the young lady in the pictures and then at the one in front of me in the wheelchair. Something struck me, but more of my revelation later. Let's just say that when I first looked at the picture I felt a lump in my throat. I pitied Eileen. The contrast between the able-bodied, cheerful young woman and the elderly lady banished to a life in a wheelchair was heartbreakingly tragic. I didn't know how she could possibly allow herself to keep such memories displayed in her house. If it were me, it would be a constant reminder of just how cruel life can be and I'd insist that all such mementos be bundled together, put on a massive bonfire and burned. I wouldn't be able to forgive the world for this. Of course, as with most of my knee-jerk assessments of situations, I was wrong.

We sat in the garden and shot the breeze. Rob was much more confident with new people than I was, so he was instantly chatting away, asking about the dog and Eileen's disability. I sat and listened, only occasionally piping up to nod, or chuckle, or say something monosyllabic. I was shy.

Eileen wasn't. She was a natural with everyone – dogs, humans, anything. She had a way of talking to me in a sweet, gentle, supportive tone, which slowly, throughout the course of the visit, melted my Concerta-addled heart and opened me up. I'd *never* met anyone who had such an effect on me. She was like an anti-ADHD pill. I just couldn't get cross or surly around her. I even swept my hair out of my face so she could take a proper look at me. In my world, that's a big compliment.

We took Sailor out for a walk, then all went for a Nando's together; there was one not far from her house, which was a bonus. I don't eat a lot of fast food – it's not great for my condition – but I can't resist some well-barbecued chicken.

'So, you've got Sailor now, but what were you doing before him?' I asked, nibbling a chip.

'Well, I had helpers doing the jobs that Sailor does. They'd come by, and if I'd dropped something they'd pick it up, or if I needed washing, they'd lend a hand; everything really.'

'Oh, right,' I said, suddenly shy again. 'Erm, cool.'

'It is cool, Liam.' Eileen chuckled. 'It's really cool.'

In the afternoon we went to the supermarket to pick up some bits and bobs, then we nipped into the butcher's to fetch some meat. Watching Eileen and Sailor was amazing. I'd literally never seen anything like it. He helped her get ready to go out, and in the supermarket it was as if he were psychic, understanding her every gesture and movement. By that time I thought I'd developed a decent understanding with Aero, but compared to these guys we were virtual strangers.

'Oh, you're such a helpful lad.' Eileen smiled as I escorted her around the aisles, making me feel like a million dollars.

It was like she could see my wow factor. It sounds corny, but she made me want to be a better person. It was like she had a PhD in positive reinforcement. She made me feel so good about every little thing I did to help that I wanted to do more. I trundled ahead down the busy street, patrolling to make sure that the pavement was clear enough for a lady in a wheelchair. I'm not quite certain why I took on this job – it probably wasn't entirely necessary, as I'm sure she'd been down the road many times – but I wanted to feel useful. I was actually enjoying helping someone.

That might have had a little something to do with Sailor – I found it a total inspiration just seeing how helpful he was. Here was Eileen, a happy soul, who deserved much better from life, and I could see that Sailor was her ray of sunshine.

He was her best pal and trotted by her side like the luckiest dog alive.

Sipping a cup of tea back at home, Eileen looked at me with a quizzical smile and asked me a direct question. 'So I hear you're a lad with problems. What's up then, Liam?'

I sat beside her and explained all my issues, and what I'd been through. I felt bad muttering on about my problems, when she was in a wheelchair, but her warmth and obvious concern made it easy to confide in her.

'You seem like a good lad to me,' she said with a smile, resting her hand affectionately on my arm.

It felt like she had instantly seen the goodness in me that most people missed.

Afterwards, she demonstrated all the ways in which Sailor helped make her life easier. We watched as he dragged her washing into the machine with his mouth, then clicked the door shut with his wet, black nose. It all made sense suddenly. These were the exact skills that I was teaching Aero. When he was doing it for me, though, it was a performance, but in this environment it was just part of the day-to-day routine – and even more important than I'd imagined.

During the course of the afternoon we did all those things that fill kids my age with absolute dread – chores. We ironed, cleaned up the house, did the washing. Yet, while I would avoid these tasks like the plague at home, to do them with Eileen was an absolute pleasure. Despite the fact that she must have an incredibly difficult life, Eileen was always quick to laugh – and to make me laugh. She was so gracious for someone in a wheel-chair, and the relationship between her and her dog, Sailor, was hilarious. It was obvious that they absolutely adored each other, yet totally understood each other too.

Seeing someone wheelchair-bound getting by with an assist-ance dog in a huge city was fascinating too. Up until now my entire experience of these miracle dogs had been against the backdrop of a rural town, or in the countryside, but seeing how the pair deftly made their way through the hustle and bustle of such a sprawling and busy city was amazing. Rob and I were lolloping behind for most of the day, slightly out of our depth. I hadn't enough experience of London to feel totally at ease, and Rob seemed to spend most of the day getting distracted; he was completely taken by the noisy guys selling fruit and veg, shouting out the price of produce in the strangest cockney voices I'd ever heard. And I'm an *EastEnders* fan. Meanwhile Eileen and Sailor zipped along, telepathically nipping into shops to pick up items quicker than any able-bodied person would be able to manage. I'd seen demonstration after demonstration over at Canine Partners, but nothing had come close to this; it was a whole level up. The pair of them had a grace about them, as if their movements were studiously choreographed. As you can probably tell, I was well impressed.

At the end of the day, the three of us sat down to talk through what we'd learned. I was eager to find out what Eileen's life had been like before she'd got an assistance dog.

'So how has Sailor changed your life?' I asked, looking at her radiant face, framed by short grey hair and dangly gold earrings glittering in the light.

'He's given me life, Liam,' she said, with a hint of sadness.

I nodded sagely, then excused myself to go to the loo, glancing at the pictures in the lounge on my way. I didn't pity Eileen, I was inspired by her. Earlier that day I had looked at those pictures and all I'd noticed was that she didn't have a disability then, but she does now. But having spent a day with her, intoxicated by her personality, I could see exactly why she kept the memories in her house. The smiling face in the pictures was precisely the same one that had greeted me at the front door earlier that morning, and had beamed throughout the day, without once tiring. Even Rob and I had flagged in the mid-afternoon, bloated with Nando's, and we were supposed to be boisterous young men. The lady in the pictures had the same spirit as the lady in the wheelchair. No tragedy in the world could destroy Eileen. Needless to say, she has quickly become my Pop Idol.

As soon as the loo door closed behind me, tears streamed down my face. Yes, proper tears. This was a breakthrough for the boy who had no real empathy or emotions. Eileen had found my heart.

I sat there crying, vowing that whatever I did for Aero in the future, I would do it in the name of this remarkable woman.

I wiped my tears away, and got ready to face my future.

Then flushed the loo.

7

The Eileen effect

I strode back into Canine Partners with serious business in
mind.

That morning I'd washed and brushed my hair, put on my
most powerful outfit – clean T-shirt, deeply fashionable blue
jeans (baggier than your average), my least smelly pair of trainers. I wanted to show my colleagues the new Liam. Not the
same lanky teenager who'd been traipsing around the grounds
for the last few weeks. Oh no, that guy had vanished about a
week ago, when I'd returned from London.

'Morning, love,' said Mum, pretending not to notice how
much I had changed. She probably felt too overwhelmed to
mention it.

The same went for the other kids on the bus. I boarded the
usual old white minibus with the red stripe down the side, but
this time I did it with an impressive air of importance. I didn't
waft aboard still half asleep as usual, before enduring half an
hour at the Rob show – which is, admittedly, very entertaining.
I made my entrance with grace and allure.

'All right, matey!' high-fived Rob as I arrived. It was, of
course, the same old childish gesture I was used to, and I'll even
admit it, I think I started the high fives in the first place. But
I was a younger man then, wet around the gills. If I'd had my
way I'd be more inclined to a nod and a handshake, but I let his
moment of frivolity pass without comment.

I wanted to talk to the others about the dogs, and how we
all needed to realize the enormous magnitude of what we were

doing. Eileen had inspired me, her dog Sailor had inspired me, and now I wanted us all to feel inspired about this stuff. In my head I had prepared a speech to rival other great inspirational talks from icons like Churchill and Obama.

Meeting Eileen had woken me up, given me that extra lightning bolt of oomph, and the whole experience had made me feel differently about my little doggy pal and the work we were doing together. This was a big deal, we were saving people with disabilities, for God's sake!

I took the sharp intake of breath necessary to launch into a tremendous speech, one that would motivate my friends, my colleagues, to join me in this quest to the highest summit, to train a legion of dogs to save lives and improve the planet, to bring smiles to those far less fortunate than ourselves. Yes, we had problems! Yes, we were society's forgotten children! Yes, we had our own mountains to climb! But we could show the world that we were here to stand proud, to aid those in need of greater assistance, to make this world better for our children, and for our children's children, and for our children's children's children's children . . . Just as I was about to say all that, I noticed that Ellie and Allie were lost in talk of nail varnish, Rob was into a magazine, and Katrina was staring mindlessly out of the window.

I'll do the speech later, I promised myself. Well, all right, not *promised*. I *suggested* to myself. Like a ship passing in the night, the moment had gone, just slipped past. It would have been a wonderful speech though. I'm sure of it.

As the months had passed at Canine Partners and I'd grown to know my new friends better, I realized that we all had totally different problems. To the naked eye, we were all the same, some kids who caused trouble in school. The big misconception was that we were just plain bad, and, like everyone else, when I laid eyes on the people in this with me, I assumed they were worth steering clear of too. But that was about a million miles away from the truth, and underneath it all they were nice teenagers, just a little bit confused like me. We were a group of kids who needed a comforting arm and a kind word, but instead we'd been treated with punishment and anger.

The more I'd learned about how to get the best out of your pets, the more I realized that exactly the same theories could be applied to us 'terrible teenagers'. The dogs in Canine Partners were treated with fun, excited voices and rewards for their good behaviour. Under school conditions, they would all be surly young pups growling in detention, feeling terrible about themselves for the things they'd done wrong. But here they were praised for the things they did right. It's simple really – if you hold a mirror in front of someone and tell them all their faults, they probably won't blossom into a kind, well-rounded human being. But if you hold up exactly the same mirror and list their qualities that are attractive or good, or even just normal, they will be fine. Like I said, we could all learn a lot from this place. I know I was.

However, I was aware that my journey wasn't the same as the other kids'. I knew that just because I had seen the light, it didn't mean that they would, and if I'd started preaching to them about what we were doing, they'd turn on me. I knew that because I'd do exactly the same if the roles were reversed. I've never been a big fan of swots. That's not my way of playing my experience up and their experiences down; I think we all came away from Canine Partners feeling positive and different about ourselves. It's simply that once we became individuals rather than another rabble of terrors, our reasons for being there were different. I needed to learn to trust my own instincts and not feel ashamed of who I was. One of my many youth workers once told me that the key to being happy and comfortable was to 'embrace the inner idiot', and the more I thought about it, the more I thought that they were probably right.

So, with my inspirational talk put to one side, I went looking for my dog to see what kind of miracles we could achieve today. After spending some time with Sailor, I knew we had plenty to work on – after all, Sailor was a superdog. I now knew what it must feel like to be the best guitar player in a school band, then jamming with the bloke from the White Stripes, and feeling totally left in the shade.

All of a sudden, Aero's skills seemed a little bit too rough around the edges. I didn't want my dog to be just half decent at this stuff, I wanted him to be the best. I wanted Aero to win Olympic gold medals at collecting laundry, answering phones, calling lifts. And right now, Sailor was the dog to beat – he was the reigning champ.

Aero must have been reading my determined thoughts, the cheeky little swine, because as I approached his kennel with an extra authoritative spring in my step, he pretended not to have noticed me. I knew that move all too well – the one when you ignore the person who may or may not be in a bad mood. I know it well because many a time I've heard Mum get home from work, and just by the sound of her footsteps I can tell what kind of mood she's in. If she's walking heavily, stomping, it's time to make myself scarce. But if her footsteps sound quick and light, she's cheerful. For me, the heavy steps would find me ducking out into the back garden to hide, or heading to the shed to draw a cartoon. Aero could sense the impatience in my movement, so he blanked me.

'Aero!' I shouted, not with the usual joy and kinship in my voice, but more in the same way that a regional manager might call for one of his staff when he wants something done.

Aero looked up at me, and strolled towards me very half-heartedly, as if to say, 'What's your problem, dipstick?' He could definitely read me.

'Sit down,' I deadpanned. And down he went, not in his usual playful manner, but in a surly way. Again, I knew the technique, as it was one I'd always reserved for headmasters when told to sit down in their office, or when ordered to take a spot right at the front of the classroom where everyone can keep a good eye on me.

'Good boy,' I almost growled. I think he shrugged. Had he been chewing gum at this point, I would have put a wastepaper basket under his chin and demanded he spit it out. But, alas, he wasn't.

It was a bittersweet moment for me and my dog, who was, let's face it, also my best pal. The division of power had never really been there before, but now it was. Big-time. It's easy to forget that for all the obvious differences between man and beast, animals are still emotional and insightful. Especially dogs and cats who are so commonplace with people. Nina had always made a point of this, and emphasized that the puppies were clever enough to read our moods, and so far I'd always been cheerful and playful with my pal. But something about meeting Sailor had shifted the balance. I was confident around Aero now, and I needed more from him.

It sounds silly, but I think that up until that point Aero had been in charge of our progress. I'm not playing down my fantastic achievements too much, but I'm man enough to accept that a lot of the success rested on the shoulders of my furry partner. As I'd sat there vulnerably and awkwardly in a rusty wheelchair nodding feverishly at a washing machine, begging with my eyes for Aero to empty it, it was Aero who picked up on what was going on, and shuffled over to take out the clothes and dollop them on the floor. He'd been the one really doing the work, and making us the successful partnership that we were. But when I saw how controlled Eileen was with Sailor, I realized that it was time for me to take the reins and lead the way. After all, Aero needs to be bossed by his future owner, not the other way around.

I knelt down, and gave him the usual playful stroke. 'I'm sorry, mate, but it's got to be serious business from now on.'

He fixed me with a glance and I knew that he understood and respected me. If he were a human being, he would have told me that he got where I was coming from, and that, damn it, he was with me all the way on this. It made me swell with pride inside, and I had to stop myself from welling up with emotional tears of determination. And then Aero went tearing off into the field, chasing a bird. Oh, man, it was going to be a long day.

'It's lunchtime, Liam!' Nina shouted over, as I went through a few simple exercises with Aero.

'I'm all right!' I gestured. 'I'll eat something in a bit.'

She walked slowly towards me as I went through some of the early drills – sit, roll over, lie down.

'What are you up to?' she asked.

'Just going through a few old routines, so that we don't forget them when we're mastering the tougher stuff. I want him to be perfect.'

'Carry on like this and he will be.' She smiled. 'Keep it up.'

I exchanged a look with Aero; he knew what I was saying. I was letting him know how good those words from Nina felt, and how I wanted more of the same. I demanded perfection. Unfortunately, such was the nature of our relationship that Aero was always game for a bit of mischief. I'd normally get bored doing whatever we were doing, so we'd have a bit of a run or a wrestle to break up the monotony. He was used to my unfocused behaviour, so it came as a shock to him when I ignored his more playful moves.

There he was in front of me bouncing up and down, demanding that I pay him attention, but we didn't have time for this right now. I so wanted him to be a commando like Sailor that I didn't want to waste a single minute we had together.

'Focus, Aero!' I snapped. He wasn't getting his treats, because I was attempting – not very well – to ignore the bad playfulness that was wasting our time. I wasn't being the Liam he'd come to know. Part of me felt really guilty about that, but deep down I knew that I needed to break him down and build him back up again, a bit like Tyra Banks does in *America's Next Top Model*, or an army drill instructor does in any number of war films. Not that I've ever watched *America's Next Top Model*, of course, I'd just noticed it from time to time when Mum had left it switched on at home. My favourite moment was when a girl was scolded because she had a great face but her 'eyebrows lack intensity'. What does that mean? No one knows. Still, there was a deeply impressive quality about Tyra's ability to destroy them then build them up – it works every time. So, to make Aero the best in the business, I needed to make him dislike me a little bit first. Take a leaf from the supermodel's book.

What I didn't acknowledge was that with Aero, hatred, or any negative emotion, doesn't even exist. You could be inches away from his face absolutely spitting venom about something, angry drops of saliva spattering his coat, and he'd still be cheerfully looking for the good in you. Or waiting for his moment to do an unbelievably cute manoeuvre, like offer a paw, as if to say 'friends?', or playfully collect a toy for you both to muck around with. Everything about my dog's nature was geared towards making the best of the day – if he was a person, he'd have a constant fixed grin, and a joke and a giggle for every occasion. He reminded me a bit of my mum like that. They're both optimists. About as far away from me in that sense as you could get.

Of course, the last thing I wanted to do was change my dog too much. Aero was my best pal just the way he was. I needed him to let me change, that's all. And the more we practised and focused, and moved forward in our mission to stand alongside Sailor and the other greats who had graduated from Canine Partners, the more our relationship seemed to morph naturally into one more akin to teacher/student than partners-in-crime. We could still monkey around with the best of them, but we knew when to get down to business too. And it didn't take too long to get to that stage, although at first Aero had reacted with bemusement at my attempts to take training a little bit more seriously.

Thanks to his kind, open nature he was friendly with all the other dogs and their owners – a trait I was quite grateful for in the earlier days. Back then I was more inclined to take an easy ride, to get through the day while expending minimal effort, so to have Aero wander off to play with some of the others, or

sniff around Rob – who he'd obviously taken a shine to as well
– was fantastic. It meant that I could slope off, knowing that
he'd be fine. I've always noticed that within relationships there
tends to be one quieter partner, and with Aero and me, as well
as Rob and me when we weren't at Canine Partners, I was the
one who took the back seat, allowing the other to sweep up
the plaudits and attention. I was far more comfortable that way,
and after years of having the attention for all the wrong reasons,
it was nice to be away from the glare of the spotlight altogether.
Aero had definitely been the star of this particular show, and he
was one of the most popular furry faces in Canine Partners. I'm
not sure the same could be said of me.

Anyway, I'd decided to change all that – to become the
dominant partner, and thankfully, like people, dogs adapt
incredibly quickly, so it wasn't long before he was up for the
ride with me, kindly allowing me to direct how we progressed.
The responsibility made me feel amazing, and I knew that it
was starting to show to everyone around.

Gone were the deliberate gestures and pleading voices; our
level of communication had reached the point of being near
telepathic. I realized this one blustery afternoon, when I was far
too freezing cold to take Aero to the field. He was full of energy,
sitting in the lobby, looking to me for guidance. He wanted to
play, I wanted to stay warm, so I decided to keep him busy with
some new games. I stood up, walked to the lift, and darted my
eyes towards the button to call it. Aero leapt up to call the lift.
I nodded towards the door to the hall, and he bounced over and
opened it up. In the hall I glanced at the washing machine, and he
was over there in a second, awaiting instruction. This was amazing. It was like he could read my face. This was a really big deal.
I ambled slowly towards the pretend cash machine in the hall,
and in nano-seconds he was next to me, ready to help me with-
draw some much-needed pretend money. 'Good boy!' I cheered,
throwing a world of treats on to the floor. He'd forgotten all
about going outside, and so had I.

'You deserve a treat,' said Mum when I arrived home. 'You're always talking about how Aero gets a treat whenever he's been good, and I think you've done so well.'

I stopped in my tracks. I was readying myself to bound upstairs to do some drawing, but this was a conversation well worth sitting down for. I tossed my bag into the corner of the lounge, and collapsed into the lower-ranking sofa. Our lounge has two comfy sofas – one that operates under a strict age-based policy, so the eldest get first dibs, and a second one with a less-welcoming softness, but not too bad none the less. Generally, when I got home from school Mum would already have claimed the decent one. I knew my place.

She turned her attention from *Deal or No Deal*. 'So what do you think would make for an appropriate treat, Liam?'

What kind of question was that? She hadn't bothered giving me any kind of parameters, and I know better than most that people like me, with my condition, need to know exactly where the limits were drawn. Could I ask for a sunshine holiday? A nice shiny pair of trainers? Could I go the whole hog and ask for a PlayStation 3? It was impossible to know.

I examined Mum's expression. She was totally serious about this, I knew, because her smile was fixed on me, and she was granting me plenty of thinking time. If it was a joke, she'd have burst out laughing by now, I assured myself.

'Take your time. I'm proud of you, Liam, and I think you're grown-up enough now to pick your own reward.'

I consulted the files in my brain dedicated to the things that other people had that I wanted. It was one of the bigger files, absolutely littered with everything from personality traits, to physical appearance, to sporting prowess, to shiny expensive items in shops. To reduce the contents of this file had become a lifetime ambition, and at that point in the lounge, staring at one another while a bearded Noel Edmonds did his usual bit in the background, I had a great opportunity to start work on it. Until I realized the truth of the situation.

'I don't need a treat, Mum, just doing what I'm doing is enough.'

She looked like she was going to cry, so I took that as an invitation to the premier-ranking sofa. We had a hug, and Mum promised to cook me my favourite that evening for tea. And so the entire family was subjected to macaroni cheese – delicious.

'I spoke to Mr Blackmore, and he said you're much better at school.' Mum beamed at me, with the whole family around the table, the others all completely aghast by what they had just heard.

'Sorry, Mum, did you just say that Liam is doing well?' joked my brother. 'Where's a film camera when you need one!'

I gave him a playful poke. 'That's enough, you lot are just jealous, and to answer your question, Mum, yes, I am amazing, so—'

'There was no question,' chirped Mum. 'I'm just proud of you, we all are.'

Dad gave me a wink, his legendary seal of approval. It felt absolutely brilliant to have my family feeling positive about me, and knowing that they could see the difference in me was wonderful.

I chuckled to myself as I sat in the garden watching the sun go down, imagining Mum talking to Mr Blackmore. I bet her heart sank at first: here we go again, more trouble from my difficult son. She would have braced herself for the worst, prepared herself for yet another half an hour of biting her lip, desperately trying to defend me, explaining that my condition sometimes makes me do terrible things. She probably thought it was a wind-up at first. 'You what? We are talking about the same Liam? Lanky, awkward, a bit lazy?' Yes, he would explain, before further blowing bubbles and tweeting about my fantastic progress. 'Liam Creed? The Liam Creed? My son?' Mum would continue to question in a loud, clear voice, like a granny trying to order afternoon tea from a French waiter on holiday.

'Yes, your Liam,' he would say, causing Mum to fall backwards, feeling a little bit faint. How fantastic.

Both Mum and Dad gave me a massive hug when I decided to call it a night. I could get used to making them feel proud of me, it felt great.

At school I was slowly starting to morph into one of those kids at the front of the class putting in their all. A good rep can buy you a whole world of peace and quiet, I had realized. Those were two features I wasn't entirely used to, but I was determined to grow accustomed to them. I made a mental note to become absolutely, amazingly brilliant at everything.

If only Aero shared a similar outlook. Our relationship was at about 'phase three' by now, which was a phase oozing with familiarity. We'd done the whole 'phase one' thing of awkwardly tiptoeing around each other trying to figure one another out, we'd drifted merrily through the 'phase two' getting-to-know-you bit, something that I believe couples call the 'honeymoon period'. Now we were at ease with one another. I could see everything that was totally great about my dog – his willingness to muck in and get his paws dirty, his constant eagerness to learn and have a ton of fun along the way. But I could also see all the little creases that needed to be ironed out – the accidental roughness when we wrestled sometimes, the preference for play over work. His boundless enthusiasm was fine when he was knocking around with me, an able-bodied teenager in pretty good shape (even if I do say so myself), but his rough and tumble could potentially be hazardous with someone in a wheelchair who couldn't match his energy. So I realized that I needed to find a way to help Aero control his enthusiasm, without losing the cheerfulness that made him such a joy to hang around with. I decided to ask Nina what she thought.

'Well, what a fantastic question,' she chirped. 'You're finally thinking outside your own sphere, that's brilliant.'

Once again, for the second time in as many weeks, my chest

inflated with pride, and stood roughly a foot away from the rest of my body. My head simultaneously swelled to about nine times its usual size. Much more of this and I was going to have to demand bigger doors in the building.

Nina explained to me that while I had bonded with Aero on a playful level, the next stage was to develop the relationship we had into one of trust and control. We could still be pals, but she said the boundaries of seriousness needed to be set too.

'It's not a million miles away from how I am with you kids.' She laughed. 'We can have fun, but you've seen my serious, strict side too, Liam. That's how grown-ups have to be.'

She was right, and I had lots to think about. I had spent the whole time thinking about the course and the training from my own perspective: how would this help me? Would I look good on telly? Even questions like 'Does Aero like me?' became important in my own head. But since my return from London, from the inspiration of meeting Eileen and Sailor, I'd formed a whole new list of questions, and for once in my life I wasn't the focus of all of them. I was in there somewhere though, naturally. I wanted to know how Aero could improve. What kind of person would he benefit? What steps did we need to take together to make the most of this whole fantastic situation that I'd been blessed with?

It was a relief not to spend the day navel gazing, and it was foreign territory too. For so long, essentially fifteen years, everywhere I'd been, it was my behaviour that had been the main focus. When I was a toddler I stood out because I was louder and more obnoxious than most normal kids; my entire school career (if you can call it that) had been spent with authorities peering over their glasses at me, trying to figure out what was wrong. Even at home I was like a trouble magnet. So, to be away from the limelight, to be just another small character in a far bigger story was an absolutely enormous relief. It was like a weight lifted from my shoulders, and I didn't feel so self-conscious any more.

That's how I began to think about it. I'd close my eyes and imagine the tragic story of someone else, someone who might have been able-bodied, but had that privilege snatched from them in a cruel twist of fate. But what they don't realize is that there is still a life left for them, and it's definitely worth living. That Aero was born to this, that Susan came along and trained him during those early days to be obedient and kind, that I was drafted in during an equally strange twist of fate – it was all meant to happen. I was meant to meet this great dog who brings out the best in me, and together we were set on a road to giving someone a new life, some independence and a massive smile just like the one Eileen had that day when she opened the door to me. I was part of a great big machine designed to make life better for people who needed a boost. That felt bloody good, I must say. Whoever gets Aero is going to have the greatest dog in the land, that's what I promised myself.

And it felt like it was starting to work, this whole crazy plan of mine. As I became more focused on the aspects of our training that I wanted to improve, Aero learned the boundaries. When he was playing up, desperate for fun when we were supposed to be working, I would turn my back to him, and he would eventually stop and just get on with the training. At first it was hard, probably a bit like hearing a baby cry and not dashing off to help it out. But pretty soon Aero was just as determined and straight-faced as me about the training. Weirdly, it made us closer. I was worried that by suddenly taking on the role of strict teacher we might lose a bit of the friendship that we had been so lucky to develop, but the opposite happened; Aero seemed more eager to see me, keener to impress me, and more affectionate when we were playing together. I know it's not the most macho admission in the world, and my friends would probably totally tear me to pieces for saying it, but Aero loved me, and I loved Aero. He had become the main focus in my life, and for that time I was the main focus in his.

Things I'd seen and not understood at the beginning of the course started to make sense – notably Susan's relationship with her dogs. She was an absolutely lovely lady, but sometimes she'd snap at little Aero (as small as he was then), but he still seemed completely smitten with her. I thought that was strange at the time – a bit like me actually liking one of my teachers – but now it made complete sense. She'd had the same relationship with the puppy Aero as I was having with the slightly older puppy version. Unlike humans, it seems, dogs like and appreciate being told what to do. It was mental note time again: be more like Aero when you're at school. Let the teachers lead you.

Now, I don't want to get too carried away with what a fantastic guy I became. Over this period of change, I still found myself in trouble at school, I still had a potty mouth when I was feeling tired, frustrated or anxious, and I was still having to dose myself up on medication every day. A miracle hadn't suddenly occurred, and I was still prone to the odd detention here and there. I think the main difference, the element that I was learning, was to try to curb the nonsense. To have some kind of control over my behaviour. What I had was a vision on the sunset to aspire towards, a sense of direction. Before all this, I was happy to barge my way through life creating a trail of destruction as I went, with nothing but chaos lying ahead of me. Now I could see where I wanted to be, I just had to get there. Next step – get a grip on girls.

8

Overcoming my fear of women, thanks to a dog!

Much as I loved Aero, I knew our relationship was strictly platonic. But what I had learned from my doggy pal was how to connect and how to empathize, even just a little bit. It might sound weird to normal people, but to have formed a recognizable bond away from home was a pretty big deal to me. It gave me a modest confidence boost that would see me switching my sights temporarily away from Canine Partners and on to a hot young should-be supermodel who was starting to have quite an effect on my day.

That's right, I'd developed a crush on a girl. She walked past me every day on her way to school. She was amazing. She had lovely long blonde hair, she dressed in girlie pink things, yet she still looked cool and rebellious – it was a vibe. I was at the boys-only school down the road, so my talking-to-girls skills were a trifle lacking. But getting to know Ellie and Allie and various other girls at Canine Partners had convinced me that girls weren't actually from Planet Zod, and that sometimes you could have a real conversation with them. If only I could transplant this knowledge outside the boundaries of Canine Partners everything would be fine and dandy. But I was still working on that.

In my daydreams I would attract this girl's attention as we passed in the street. Then I would regale her with a funny story about something that had happened to me the day before – I've heard that girls rank a sense of humour highly – and follow it up by smoothly asking her out for a milkshake/cocktail some time. She would, of course, giggle coyly and tell me that she'd seen me around for absolutely ages and was hoping that one day I might stop and talk to her. She'd tell me that she just so happens to think milkshakes are brilliant too, especially the ones with malt in them, and that sharing one sounds fantastic. We'd casually exchange numbers, she'd kiss me on the cheek in front of loads of kids from my school, and then off I'd strut, probably the coolest man who ever lived.

I'd taken to speaking to Aero about this on a regular basis during our mid-morning stroll, and, unlike people, he never seemed to tire of me going over and over the same questions; he just listened cheerfully to my droning.

'You know, it's not like I'm scared of girls, Aero.' I chuckled, stroking him absent-mindedly, pretending to be brimming with confidence. Oh, who was I kidding! Confiding in a whisper, I told my dog, my most trusted pal: 'Okay, I'm a little bit scared, between you and me, but you know me, and you like me, right?'

I knew he did. And I was sure that I just needed to work on my conversational skills, because, having heard them, I knew that girls liked to natter. Chatting to a dog was all well and good, but they don't have the same capacity to surprise that people have.

Unfortunately, my ability to talk to women hadn't improved much. While I was less tongue-tied than I used to be and my blushing had subsided, these traits could still hit me unawares. Ellie, Katrina and Allie were 'safe', but I could fall apart around most other girls.

So the reality was that I spent most mornings pretending not even to notice my dream girl. It was the same every day. I'd walk from my house, down the hill, along the high street, I'd nip into the newsagent's for a drink or some gum, then, turning the corner, there she would be. Every single day, at almost exactly 8.20 a.m. What she didn't realize as I zipped past with my eyes fixed firmly on my feet, my cheeks already burning ever so slightly, was that she was the high point of my day. Just seeing her made me feel great, and on the rare occasions when we didn't pass each other in the morning, I'd feel a little bit glum. Deep down I knew that this was the girl for me. I liked the fact that she was always on her own. I was always on my own too.

Of course, ideally I would have had someone I could ask about this kind of stuff, but I'd have felt weird asking Mum about it, my sister would absolutely destroy me with laughter, and I couldn't bear to think what kind of advice Ellie and Allie might dish out. I had no choice, there was only one place to find out about these strange and foreign creatures: in magazines – namely the magazines left strewn about the house, Mum's *Woman's Own*, Sophie's *Bliss* or *More*.

They were eye-opening to say the least. 'Ten Ways to Make Him Your Dream Date!'; 'Get That Guy Without Even Trying'; '48,000 Methods of Making Yourself Irresistible'.

I studied these magazines like they were library books – in secret of course. On more than one occasion, I'd have a copy of *Bliss* tucked inside a maths or science book to make it look like I was doing homework.

I'd seen swarms of girls reading similar magazines on the bus and in shops, so I figured it was safe to assume that they all read them, and the tips I was getting were absolutely priceless. Apparently girls don't necessarily want guys who look like they're in a boy band with abdominal muscles and cheekbones, they like boys who are quirky and funny. That was the general gist anyhow.

'How to Kiss Like an Expert', read one headline. What the hell was a kissing expert? I thought. Is that really a job? Had these people even thought of that? No matter, I wanted to be one, so read the article with the intensity of a forensic police officer examining a corpse.

Some days I smuggled the handy bits of literature with me to Canine Partners, and during our breaks from training I'd sit in the field playing fetch with Aero with one eye, and skim-reading an article about which chat-up lines work and which ones don't with the other eye. If I stumbled across a particularly fascinating article, I'd read it aloud to my dog to get his seal of approval.

'Hey, Aero, how about this?' I yelled, clearing my throat to make sure he digested every single word. 'Dear Agony Aunt, there's a boy in my class who I really fancy, but I'm too scared to ask him out on a date, just in case he laughs at me and makes me look stupid. It sounds silly, but it's causing me lots of sleepless nights. What should I do?'

It was like it was written for me, only the other way round. My problem was a chick, this girl's problem was a guy. It's all troubles of the heart. Aero was staring at me, mouth open, his breath heavy and expectant, as if he were actually interested in the problem page I was reading to him. If nothing else, this dog of mine was absolutely brilliant at feigning interest. I picked up the ball and threw it for him to fetch, while still insisting on reading the agony aunt's reply out loud to him, in a slightly shouted voice, just in case he really was interested and was pretending not to be. The ball zoomed off, Aero storming after it into the distance. I was miles away yelling girlie problems after him. I paused for a moment to check for cameras. This was part of my Canine Partners experience that I didn't especially want them to catch on film.

'Well, first, don't worry,' it read, 'there's no point. If we all spent our lives fearing embarrassment, none of us would ever get anything done.'

That was a good point from Agony Aunt; we really wouldn't get anything done, and I certainly wouldn't have ventured out of my house and come to train dogs to look after people with problems bigger than mine. This advice was just the ticket. I continued reading.

'My advice would be to take the bull by the horns and get to know this boy. Don't just go straight up to him and ask him for a date – perhaps start by paying him a compliment about his clothes, and see where things go from there. Remember, if he's the one for you, he won't want to make you look silly, so if he does, it just goes to prove that you're too good for him. If he is the one for you, things will go swimmingly and you'll be holding hands and snogging in no time. Good luck.'

Wow, more kissing; how did they manage to shoehorn that in there? Obviously I needed to be an expert if this relationship was ever going to work out, and so far I'd got off with a grand total of nought women, but, then again, I was at an all-boys school and not much kissing went on. Not on my watch anyhow.

'What are you reading, Liam?' asked Mum later that evening as I sat cross-legged on the sofa, utterly engrossed. They weren't used to seeing me quite so silent. In fact, between Aero and my obsession to understand women, I must have seemed much calmer, as most of the time I was completely preoccupied by my new passions. Dogs and women.

'Nothing!' I yelped, scurrying upstairs to learn more.

I was determined to become skilled in the art of kissing, although one article went into pretty off-putting detail, turning what was meant to be a pleasurable activity into something unbearable. However, another piece suggested practising on your arm or hand, so I did exactly as it instructed, and spent weeks making out with my arm. All in the name of research, you understand.

Around that same time I started to notice that Aero might be after a little bit of love too. He was a sociable dog, and great with the bitches. He was popular and charming, two qualities I could only dream of possessing, so I decided to examine his behaviour around other dogs, and see if there was any way I could adapt similar methods for my own social/love life. This no doubt sounds completely bananas to normal people, but Aero was my best pal, and as good a point of reference as any. After all, we're all animals really; our methods of communication, as human beings, are a little bit more sophisticated, but at their root not a million miles away from a gang of dogs getting to know each other. In fact, if anything, dogs are just more confident, less complex and more direct versions of people. Only with lots of fur.

Aero was always in the thick of things, playing, yapping and being generous with his peers. If bowls were being shared he'd happily budge up to accommodate another, or even patiently wait his turn. He was smiley and decent-spirited, so I made a mental note to try being a little like that myself. I just needed to get my stunning mystery woman to notice me first, then I'd dazzle her with my kindly, Aero-like nature. I was debating whether I should try doing what Agony Aunt suggested and kick off with a compliment. What would Aero do if he could speak? I think he would go for something positive and flattering. I had much to ponder before I made my move, but one thing was for certain: a move was going to be made. I'd made an oath. To myself. One evening.

'So what's her name?' asked Mum, just because I'd put on some aftershave.

'I don't know,' I snapped defensively. 'What? What are you talking about, Mum? No idea what you're on about . . . strange question . . . honestly . . . tsk . . .'

I'd probably over-egged it a touch. Plus I'd gone exactly the same colour as the curtains in my bedroom. Red.

'Oooh, there is someone! How did you meet her?'

'What? No! No, I haven't.'

'What's she into?'

'I have no idea.'

'Is she a girlie girl?'

'A what? Who? Oh, Mum, please stop it!'

'What kind of guys does she go for?'

'Hopefully ones like me,' I suddenly yapped, defeated. Damn woman and her silly mind tricks.

Mum looked at me with her head cocked sideways as if to say, 'Aw, look at my boy.' She ruffled my hair, much in the same way as I might Aero's when he's surprised me with something particularly impressive. I was starting to see doggy training parallels everywhere, it seems.

'She's a girl I see most days on my way to school, and I'm too shy to say anything, but I really want to,' I yammered nervously.

Yet, strangely, it felt brilliant finally telling someone about this secret obsession that was making me giddy. Aero had been a great sounding board and all that, but to have someone know exactly what I was on about – it was a relief of sorts.

'Girls love compliments,' gushed Mum, happy to help her boy. 'And it's flattering if a boy starts off with a positive comment about how you look.'

'Oh yeah, I know that already.' I sat up, enthused. 'I read that in . . . um, somewhere.'

I wasn't ready to pass on my secret magazine obsession. Not yet. Thankfully, Mum was too busy thinking of gems to pass on to her son that she totally missed my almost slip.

'Are you talking about girls?' said Dad, suddenly appearing in the room as if from nowhere. 'It's a sign of confidence if you make the first move to say hello,' he said, nodding at me sagely, as if to tell me to listen to him, not my mum. 'It shows that you're comfortable with who you are – women love that.'

I nodded at Dad, darted my head to Mum, as the pair hit me with information, left, right and centre. If I'd had a pen handy I would have been keenly taking notes; this stuff was gold. Pure gold. My brain was being crammed with years' worth of learning and facts, and, for his part, Dad was pretty good, but Mum was excellent. This was their chance to pass on their knowledge, a bit like I was doing with Aero. It was invigorating. I could understand why people and animals can get a thirst for knowledge. I just wished that I could feel the same passion about some of my classes at school. Suddenly my all-boy education seemed totally ridiculous. We need a female perspective. In fact, how about girls' magazines and dogs available in every all-boys school in the country? That would make the world a better place, I'm sure of it.

From that point on, Mum and Dad continued to educate me in the ways of women as often as they could – some days completely against my will. Most of their advice was fantastic, some of it was completely overwhelming.

'Don't be too available, but don't be unavailable either.'

What did that mean? Even Einstein wasn't that cryptic.

'Liam, seriously, take my advice, if you really want her to like you, make out that you don't like her,' Dad said with a wink one evening. 'Girls, like us guys, enjoy a challenge.'

'No, you're wrong, don't listen to him, Liam – you've got to be nice to girls, that's what we really respond to,' countered Mum.

It was like having an angel on one shoulder and a devil on the other, only I didn't know who was who. On balance, Mum was probably the more angelic of the two (I do, of course, have to say that).

'Be scruffy, it's more manly.'

'Wrong! We like guys who have made an effort!'

'Go halves, it's rude and old-fashioned to pay for everything.'

'Always pay.'

'Treat her *mean*.'

'Treat her.'

My mind was whirring! This was relationship advice with ADHD. I appreciated all the words of wisdom, but it was a lot to take in.

But confusing or not, this was the stuff I needed to hear! My confidence was growing, not just because of their unbelievable relationship wisdom, but because I was spending more time learning about girls without feeling like I was the only person in the whole world who didn't understand them. It was a weight lifted from my shoulders not to feel so cripplingly self-conscious.

It also helped that four of the latest additions to my life – Aero, Rob, Nina and Eileen – were all so proud to be who they were, warts and all. I'd spent years hiding behind a surly mask, desperately avoiding eye contact with the rest of the world. I didn't want people to see who I was underneath it all, because I didn't want to feel so exposed. I was short-changing myself, and I was short-changing all the people who did have faith in me. But spending time around people so unashamed to be stupid, or to make fools of themselves – even Rob, despite his reputation as something of a loose cannon – was absolutely inspiring. They threw their personalities out there, and couldn't care less what anyone thought of them. It made them infectious, and just being with any of those four for any stretch of time made me feel more comfortable about myself. They were good people, and they all had time for me, so if they could see something worthwhile about me, there must be something in there somewhere. In terms of where this put me with the quest to woo the love of my life, it had given me the boost I needed.

The time had come to make a move. With renewed vigour I took to my usual walking-to-school route and considered operation 'woo dream girl', formulated over weeks of study, plotting and scheming. Mum and Dad had told me in no uncertain terms that I must stop looking down at my feet when passing the woman who had my heart. I needed to establish eye contact. That would apparently lead to familiarity, which would, in turn, lead to casual greetings, which would one day escalate into a full-blown relationship.

On my next day at Canine Partners, with all the advice swimming around in my brain, I needed to clear my head, so I strolled down to the kennel, and asked my pal Aero if he fancied a walk. Of course, in the human world that would probably take words and noises, but I just needed to nod at Aero for him to know what was up. He grabbed his leash with his teeth and trotted over. Without a sound I clipped on the leash as if it were second nature – no wrestling moves, no struggling, just pure habit – and off we strolled in the direction of the great outdoors. Every so often I would take time to think about how far we had come, me and my dog, and I'd give myself an imaginary pat on the back. If Liam from day one could see how casually I went about leashing up Aero, he'd probably have passed out. I hate to admit it, but I was becoming seriously impressive. I just needed to convince this girl of that.

Aero was great, but so far, other than watching how he related to the other dogs, his relationship advice hadn't been up to much. That said, sometimes his woofs made more sense to me than what Mum and Dad were telling me; over time, they had become a little bit too competitive about giving me the best advice, so would often end up making me more confused than anything else. As a result, Aero became more important to me as a good sounding board to untangle my brain. Without him, I'd look like a lunatic strolling around a field nattering to himself. Not a good look. But today his woofs of wisdom were pure gold.

'Girls, Aero, eh! What are they about?' I boomed dramatically, looking down at my pal, pulling a face that said, 'What can you do, eh?'

He looked up at me, and rolled his eyes. He didn't get them either, or, at least, that's what he wanted me to think. I'd seen him schmoozing around the kennels, quietly playing the field. He was a bit of a Lothario.

'I mean, what am I supposed to do? Just go up to her and start talking?'

Again, Aero looked up at me. These silly little problems and dilemmas were no doubt completely lost on him; he'd be over there in a second with cocktails already mixed and poured were he a human, but he was kind enough to indulge me as he made a good attempt at a Gallic shrug. Perhaps he was having relationship issues too? I certainly hadn't noticed Aero hanging around with any other specific dogs recently. He was a bit of a social butterfly really, always nodding and chatting with pretty much everyone. I made a mental note to help him out with his love life and discover whether any of the other dogs seemed keen; he might need the kind of prods and pokes of encouragement that others had been giving me over the last few days.

'So what do you reckon, should I ask her for a date?'

He yapped at me. I took that as a yes. He'd made up my mind for me, and, honestly, how hard could it really be just to talk to a stranger? I'd spent big portions of my life talking to strangers in white coats, and this one was no different – just prettier, and not quite so medical.

I put together a foolproof plan, and decided to start with a simple nod, greeting and a well-placed compliment the next time I saw her. Easy.

Or so I thought. The morning came for the big introduction. I'd decided to do it on a Monday morning, so that I had the weekend to prepare, and I had practised all through Saturday on unattractive strangers I'd passed during the day – mainly old women on the high street. Most of them said a cheerful 'hello' back, one or two did look slightly bemused by the lanky teen barking, 'All right, I like your cardigan!' at them, but they were in a massive minority, scurrying away, clutching their cardigans as though I were out to pilfer them.

That morning I made sure I woke up extra early to prepare myself. She might have been a girlie girl, but I didn't want to look too polished. That said, I knew that it was important to make an effort. I'd seen all those guys on those hair adverts who clearly spent hours making themselves look suitably dishevelled and nonchalant. I used a few of the grooming tech-niques that I learned from Canine Partners, checking my teeth, vigorously shampooing my hair. Unfortunately the only outfit I had to work with was my school uniform, and there was only so cool you could look in a pea-green jacket, a white shirt, a silly tie and some humiliating slacks. I decided to go for big boots for footwear – they gave me the look of a motorcycle rebel, a classic, sexy look, no? – and I squeezed my tie further into the smallest knot possible and tucked it into my shirt. My jacket hung down from my shoulders, as if moments away from tum-bling to the floor. This was definitely the look; no girl would be able to resist this vision of teenage adolescence. I fashioned my hair to give the impression that I might have slept rough in a hedge, a style that Aero particularly thrives on.

For a brief pause, I wondered whether I should carry my brother's skateboard to create the illusion of being a hip and trendy skater. I thought better of it when I had a frightening daydream in which she is so overcome with awe at the sight of the board that she demands I perform all my best moves immediately, only for me to kick-flip my way into the middle of the road, where a juggernaut smashes into me like a tennis racket pulverizing an ant. I didn't especially want that to happen. So I opted to have my sketchbook hanging from my backpack instead. That way, if we got chatting and I was running out of things to say, I had a prop. I could talk her through a few of my favourite cartoons, or I could show her my impressive line of pencil sketches of a dog called Aero, and then we could do some decent heavy-duty kissing.

I practised my nod in the mirror. I'd seen it a million times in films where some loser stares into a mirror pretending to talk to a girl, and on the morning in question I was that loser. At first I couldn't figure out whether to smile or to flirt, but once I'd seen my attempts at flirting reflecting back at me, I knew a smile was the only real option. Plus all those magazines had taught me that a cheerful, friendly boy was about ten times more appealing than a pouty one on first impressions anyway. I had noticed, incidentally, that throughout their tuition the magazine articles had contradicted themselves zillions of times – treat them mean, but always smile, be keen, but not too keen etc. – which made me think that perhaps people don't really know what they want. Anyway, that's by the by. I looked excellent, I was going to stride past, nod and attempt some kind of greeting. Usually I'd go for 'all right', so I decided to stick to the one I was most comfortable with. Followed, of course, by a sensually delivered compliment about how great she looked in whatever she happened to be wearing.

I stepped out of the house, and I could already feel my heart pounding through my shirt. I had never been so terrified in my whole life. My palms felt sweaty, I had a mild tingling sensation all over and thought I might faint. I took a deep breath, puffed out my chest, and decided to embrace the inner idiot and go with it. I had come this far, and I had put so much effort into planning this. My fright was just another obstacle, no differ- ent to the thousands of obstacles Aero and I had been forced to overcome in the last couple of months. My dog had made me realize that I wasn't a total loser if I put my mind to it, so I made a concerted effort to ignore the negative whispering voices that lurked somewhere in the murky backwaters of my mind. Thank goodness I'd remembered to take my medication too, or else I'd have been all over the place. Stress and ADHD are not the best combination in the world.

I trod the usual route to school, only this time around it felt like I had huge chunks of lead in my boots, weighing me down, causing my feet to drag. Every step felt heavy, and my mind was spinning. If this is what true love feels like, no wonder people go completely bonkers. What made it all the weirder was that I was just doing exactly the same as I did every day – only riddled with nausea and anxiety. I made it down the road, suc- cessfully navigated myself to the high street, and even managed to get into the local shop without suddenly vomiting my fear all over the counter. My mind was absolutely racing as I looked around feverishly for something to buy. I decided, through the demented haze, that chewing gum would be wise, in case everything went shockingly well.

I wished for a moment that I'd had Aero with me; he'd know how to calm me down, and would probably just yap at me and tell me to snap out of it. She's only a girl, for heaven's sake, he'd tell me. I closed my eyes and took in the longest breath I had ever, um, taken in. In my mind I pictured myself in the field reading problem pages to Aero. I simply needed to relax. Why was I panicking? No need to panic, I told myself. Oh, God, this was horrible. I hoped in that moment that true love wouldn't always feel this weird.

I was sweating, so I bought a bottle of water to down in one as well. I needed to replace the fluids, and fast. I threw my money on the counter, and the shopkeeper looked wearily at me.

'Thanks,' he deadpanned.

And off I went, perfectly terrified and completely unprepared for the challenge that lay literally around the corner. I knew the schedule, I was timing it perfectly, she would definitely be there. And, of course, as the planets aligned and the gods decided that it was indeed time for me to come face to face with my destiny, she was.

She walked towards me in slow motion, like they do in romantic films. The wind was probably blowing through her tousled hair. I can't entirely remember, it was all a bit hazy, and I felt very woozy. I was rooted to the spot, my mind totally empty; a bit of gum dropped from my mouth, while my eyelids drooped oddly, curtaining my eyes. And still she kept on coming towards me, every feature of her face pronounced, dazzling and spectacular, like a well-groomed poodle, or the planet's cutest puppy. From the small details I can just about piece back together from the most surreal morning of my life, she was wearing some very pink and glittery eye make-up. She looked drop-dead gorgeous and amazing. I looked like something someone had dragged in on their Doc Marten boot. I wanted to look at my feet and scurry past as usual, but she had me locked in and I couldn't take my eyes off her. Every muscle had tightened and I could only stand there, a freakish teenage statue staring open-mouthed like a lunatic.

She drew ever closer, and I could see by her face that she had noticed me too. Her expression became more inquisitive and disgruntled the nearer she came.

'All right!' I bellowed. Unfortunately I was so nervous that my throat had tightened, so I really had to force it to get the word from my mouth. 'I really like your jacket, it's excellent!' It flew out at roughly six times louder than the ideal volume I was going for. Worse still, it sounded a little bit aggressive and threatening. I coughed and spluttered afterwards. My throat felt dry, and my mouth had the same texture as coarse sandpaper. 'Your shoes are cool as well, they go with the jacket very nicely indeed!'

In the plan, this was the point at which she would stop and we might embark on some kind of cheerful conversation about how it really hadn't taken her that long to throw together today's outfit, and how she thought that my teenage biker look was really working too, especially with fashion being as it is today – all about teenage bikers (presumably). Then, in the best case scenario, we might decide to skip school and run away to get married and have an exciting life zipping from place to place in a snazzy convertible car with the hood down or zooming around lakes on one of those weird water motorbike things. Plus, of course, our loyal dog Aero would be in the back seat, or precariously hanging off the back of a jet-ski.

Or, in the worst case scenario, she would smile and say, 'Hello, thanks for noticing the effort I've made,' but not stop. I'd prepared myself for that. It would sting a little, but it wouldn't be so bad, and at least I'd finally have had some sort of dialogue with her, if only minimal. In dog-training terms, it would be the equivalent of strapping on a leash. Once that was on, we could proceed to walking, sitting, playing fetch. Metaphorically speaking, of course. I didn't want to put a leash on her. Not yet anyway. The point being that, to my mind, this couldn't fail. As is so often the case, however, I was wrong.

What I hadn't prepared myself for was the horrified look of disgust on her face as she strode past me in complete silence. I followed her with my eyes as she walked past totally appalled, and watched as she stomped down the street. She even turned around to have a second look at the idiot who had just yelled at her for no apparent reason. In dog-training terms, this was the equivalent of not only failing to put a leash on a dog, but watching in horror as the pup in question bound on to a nearby motorway during hurricane season. I hadn't done well. No treats for me.

Worse still, I can't even repeat what she yelled back at me as she hotfooted down the street and away from me. It's far too rude, and I'm desperately trying not to swear. But the gist was a question about what I might be looking at.

She was a feisty girl, that's for sure. And while this was a new high entry in the list of terrible experiences that I'd endured in my fifteen years and counting, a strange feeling of relief washed all over me. I'd done it, I'd said hello to a girl. All right, she'd not reacted quite as I'd hoped, in fact, not anywhere near how I'd hoped. My cool, casual demeanour had been replaced by an awkward teenage boy shouting loud, aggressive salutations at beautiful girls in the street, but, really, who cares? I'd done it. For once I hadn't shuffled past with my head down, I'd attempted to start a dialogue. I was proud of myself, in the same way that I was proud of myself on that training day many moons ago when Aero sat down without me having to sit on him first. The process had been clumsy and unappealing, but the results didn't feel totally crushing. I'd at least heard what she sounded like when she was firing swear-words at people at top volume. I couldn't wait to tell Mum and Dad what had happened so that I could get their take on it. In the short term, I would also need to figure out a new route to school.

I thought it might be high time to invest in a bike.

On my next visit to Canine Partners I decided to consult Aero.

'She told me where to go, in not so many words,' I told Aero with a chuckle as we loafed around in the kennels, me hands in pockets, him nonchalantly scanning for creepy-crawlies. I dropped a treat on to the floor in a bid to find grace with the insect world. He snorted, and then went for the doggy treat with gusto, impressively sweeping it up as if it were just a vapour and he was one of those strange ant-eaters with the big long noses. Aero could make very quick work of treats; he was getting bigger.

'Do you think that means she might like me a little bit?' I mumbled, having detailed my dubious encounter to a dog. He stopped moving, and sat in silence, not giving me any indication that he knew the answer to my question. Well, it was the big one, I suppose. It was nice to vocalize my thoughts though. For so many years I'd gone through life keeping all these insecurities and questions in my head, but hearing myself work through them put things in perspective. It didn't seem like quite such a big deal. In fact, it all felt rather funny really. Even so, I didn't want to bore Aero to smithereens, so maybe I would be wiser to run these matters by Mum and Dad?

They told me not to give up, it was a salvageable situation, and that I shouldn't let one bad experience stop me from trying again.

'What have you got to lose?' said Dad.

He was right. I could have said 'pride', but we all know that I don't have a great amount of that. However, a bit more thought was required for my next strategy. This was obviously going to be a hard nut to crack, so I'd need to hit her with an almighty charm offensive. I'd have to practise harder to get this one right and I decided that patience was the key. Luckily, having to lollop behind Aero for two months, sweeping up his trail of destruction, I'd learned a thing or two about being patient.

Of course, that wouldn't always have been the case. Not so long ago, this girl situation would have hit me much more severely, and it would probably have found me aggressively storming around the house, frustrated with the world as usual. I'd have felt bitter or angry or somehow hard done by, and I'd pity any pretty daffodils that got in my way; grown-up Liam could still destroy a nice flowerbed if the urge took him. But now, mature as I could be, I could see a little bit of me in her, if that makes sense. She was a bit of a loner too, and I understood her angry reaction to me, because I'd reacted in exactly the same way to people a million times before. In fact, I'd probably have gone even further with my outburst. She was just shy. I wasn't scared of awkwardness any more. After all, Aero had once been a stranger, and now look at the two of us having a great time together. Something deep down inside me knew that I could make my dog into Sailor and make the strange blonde girl my girlfriend while I was at it. I just didn't quite know how.

I needed another reason to say hi; the walking-past-her business didn't really strike a chord with her. Plus she probably walked past loads of guys in her day-to-day life. I was taller than most of them, which I'd hoped would make me stand out, but my height wasn't much of a talking point, unless she wanted to ask me what the weather was like up there, or something equally hilarious. I needed to do some detective work. I needed to find out if any of the three women I knew – Ellie, my sister, nan – were familiar with her.

For about six seconds it looked like my sis might come through on this one.

'Blonde hair, you say?'

Pause.

'No, I don't know her.'

But I needn't have worried about any of that stuff because, luckily for me, the gods were just fixing themselves to intervene, finally align the planets for me, and offer my woman to me on a plate. In a way.

It had been a normal day at school, or what had become more and more usual for me. A couple of months ago, it would have been a really weird day. I'd avoided trouble, kept my head down, and played the day out like an average Joe. Just blending in was my new thing, and everyone pretty much left me alone. I was strolling home, hands in pockets, kicking a pebble down the road. Along the high street, I nipped into the newsagent's and picked up a comic to copy the pictures from. That's how I practised my drawing. I went up the hill, past the park. Or, at least, I would have made it past the park had I not been distracted by the sound of a dog barking. My ears pricked up; that sounded like a Labrador retriever if I wasn't very much mistaken – not dissimilar in mischievous tone to Aero. My eyes darted left to see what the little fella was up to, and to check that it wasn't Aero enjoying a day away from Canine Partners. It wasn't, it was an older, bigger Lab. He was playfully wrestling for a toy with his owner, who just so happened to be a leggy blonde in fantastic eye make-up, with a gorgeous jacket and wonderful shoes.

Yes, it was *her*.

My face almost collapsed in a mixture of surprise and gratitude. As usual, my heart walloped against my ribcage, and I damn near burst into sweats. In a good way, you understand.

Not only was she an attractive loner like me, she was also a dog lover. This was a real turn-up for the books.

Now, back in the day, I would have been straight over there thanks to the filter problems in my mind that have trouble ignoring my impulses. I'd be standing in front of her by now, chewing through words, probably blushing with desperation, obliterating any chance of a future together. But I had a plan. If this really was the one for me, I needed to play the long game, and not dash in and mess it all up. So I took another big breath – I was getting good at those – and resisted the temptation to make a hash of it and went home.

Further detective work began. I'd already ditched the old route to school, opting instead to go earlier, missing out on the 8.20 a.m. meet-and-not-greet, so I thought the best plan was to bite the bullet and occasionally walk past her again in the morning. I wouldn't attempt the greeting, that had fallen flat, but I would be seen often enough to become a vaguely familiar face. Hopefully, after a while, she'd forget that I was the weirdo yapping at her in the street. As for the afternoons, after school, it seemed that she was a park regular. How I hadn't noticed this before was beyond me. Her dog looked like Aero's bigger, even scruffier brother.

I wasn't the most sociable child at the best of times, but interacting with Nina, Ellie and the various other females making up a large portion of Canine Partners had opened my eyes as to how normal and easy it could be to talk to girls. They weren't so different. Plus, spending time with Aero had obviously brought out my 'sensitive side' – as Mum calls it – so I'd say I was slowly morphing into the perfect guy. The big obstacle was breaking the ice. I'd already made a pig's ear of the first impression, so I knew I had lots of work to do to banish that from her mind. I thought it best to use my experience with my dog to my advantage.

'Can I give your Labrador retriever a treat?' I stammered the next time I bumped into her in the park. It wasn't smooth, but it was a start. I'd been sure to put an impressive emphasis on the words 'Labrador' and 'retriever' so that she could instantly conclude that I wasn't just some guy with a crush trying to chat her up, I was a dog lover.

'Excuse me?' She looked at me, not quite disgusted like before, more a little confused. Obviously she wasn't used to lanky teenagers asking her questions.

'I'm sorry, that probably sounded really weird.' I chuckled, attempting to put her at ease, scraping my fringe away from my eyes. 'I work with dogs and have a couple of treats in my pocket. I thought I might as well get rid of them.'

She smiled at me. 'Yeah, that's fine.'

I knelt down and handed the tasty little objects to her dog, and gave him a good solid stroke while I was at it. He was quite a bit bigger than Aero, but seemed to have the same cheerful air of playfulness about him.

I checked his teeth, as Nina had taught me all those months ago, then even looked into his ears like I was a vet inspecting him. She appeared completely comfortable with that, and, dare I say it, she even seemed a little bit impressed by the hunky dog lover in front of her whose fringe was no longer covering his eyes. This was much more like it.

'Great dogs, Labrador retrievers,' I mused. 'What's his name?'

'He's called Malcolm.' She smiled. 'Don't ask me why, it's a ridiculous name for a dog.'

'I've got exactly the same dog, but mine's called Aero,' I chirped. 'Well, not exactly the same obviously, he's a bit smaller . . . My name's Liam by the way.'

'You're kidding! My name's Lian.' She grinned back at me.

And that signalled the beginning of my initiation into the world of boyfriends and girlfriends. How could we not get together? We both loved dogs, we both found other people rather confusing, and we were one letter away in the alphabet from having exactly the same name. This felt like destiny, and it was something I would have been totally incapable of a few short months earlier. I wasn't just learning to be comfortable with my puppy, I was becoming even more comfortable in my own skin. I would often pause to consider whether when Mr Blackmore put me forward for Canine Partners he knew that it would have such a profound effect on me – or was he simply looking to get me off his back for a while? I wouldn't blame him if he had been.

My dates with Lian started by meeting in the park as often as we could. I'm not sure if she realized they were dates, but that's just details. I'd always have a little treat for Malcolm on me, and every so often I'd muster the courage to pick up a treat for Lian from the newsagent's on the way – most of the time it would be a small item like some sweets, or a can of Coke. After all, while I was obviously becoming a grown-up, I didn't have any actual money to speak of. I made her a compilation of my favourite tunes, which she never gave me a great deal of feedback on. I concluded that Nirvana is probably boy music. She was more into Sugababes and Girls Aloud.

Our relationship progressed and I learned that kissing was every bit as good as I'd hoped. We did quite a lot of it, much of the time while Malcolm sniffed around at our feet, desperate for more attention. I'd have done the same in his shoes. I kept Aero posted throughout the early days, musing during our mid-morning strolls about how matters were advancing. There was a cheerful vibe in the air. I can honestly say that life hadn't ever been this good. Remember how I looked out of the window in the vet's that time and felt jealous of all the kids bounding happily down the street on a gorgeous summer afternoon? Now

I felt like I was finally one of those kids. I might have been on meds, but I was a whisker away from feeling like I fitted in. I can't emphasize how much of a big deal that was for me.

Needless to say, my new relationship added yet another coil to the growing spring in my step. We shared a stolen moment every morning on the way to school, which guaranteed that I'd turn up at class already cheerful and ready to make the best of the day. Mum says that she'd never seen me happier, and she was right. I'd told Lian all about Aero and what we were working towards at Canine Partners, and she seemed really impressed. We were young teenagers, but it was like I had a job to be proud of, and her approval made me even more determined to do well.

I'd started doing pretty brilliantly at school too. And I was making real progress with Aero and I'd snared myself a girl-friend, a first kiss, and some important style tips – she taught me all about moisturizing and general grooming. I had to pinch myself on a daily basis to check that all this was real.

'Seriously, Aero, you have to meet her,' I chirped. 'She's great, and she's got a dog called Malcolm who's just like you only bigger.'

He yapped, obviously not keen on the idea of this bigger Malcolm.

'Okay, not much bigger. He's fully grown anyway, while you're still growing. I think you will be bigger eventually . . .'

And with that I launched a tennis ball three miles into the air as Aero hurtled off to grab it. It was at that moment that I made a promise to myself: I was going to teach that dog to catch a Frisbee in his mouth if it was the last thing I did. It just looked so much cooler.

We might have a serious job to do. But there was always room for the fun stuff.

It's about getting the balance right.

9

The big scary stage show

As the weeks hurtled by, I became aware that we were working towards something – our graduation show, to be held at
my school hall one evening, no less. As my training sessions
with Aero came to resemble a montage from a Rocky film –
lots of sweating, shouting, hugging, high fives, chest bumping,
leashes and washing machines – the reality of the final show
started to weigh heavily on my mind. I might have overcome
my crippling shyness issues in small group situations, but the
thought of being alone on a stage, just me and my dog, gave
me a funny sensation in my stomach. It was a mixture of terror,
anguish, excitement and diarrhoea. I knew that we had the
demonstration nailed, because we'd been honing it relentlessly
for weeks.

Our segment was going to feature me flawlessly placing
myself in a second-hand wheelchair and forcing my furry pal to
fetch my laundry from a full washing machine, which would be
situated somewhere in the vicinity of stage left. Both of us could
do this bit with our eyes closed now. I barely needed even to
gesture, just clicks and claps, and encouragement – Aero knew
what my eyes were saying. Of course, I'd need to ham it up a bit
for the big show, otherwise it might look like I wasn't actually
doing anything at all. I'd say 'good boy' and 'that's it' and 'come
on, Aero' a lot, and at the end I'd scatter a handful of tasty treats,
bow to the crowd as they stood on their chairs enraptured by
the show, clapping so hard that their hands would be swollen
and bruised by how brilliant I was. Plus, of course, Lian and

Mum would be there weeping with pride. In fact, even a tough guy like Mr Blackmore would probably be moved to tears.

Although most of that wasn't actually going to happen. Lian wasn't coming – I'd made that decision for her. So far I'd taken to my first real-life relationship with some style and sensuality, but I didn't want to ruin everything by having a humiliating public breakdown and losing my sex appeal – assuming that I had some. So she was barred from the big hall, just in case. Allowed to watch were my family, Mr Blackmore, and a handful of friends and relatives belonging to other members of the group and Canine Partners. In total, there would probably be about a hundred people watching, but with the added whirring cameras taking in the whole show, I did some basic speculative maths and came up with a figure nearer to the 7 million mark. It was, understandably, causing me sleepless nights.

Aero, on the other hand, was lapping it up – he was a showman, made for the stage. In the last couple of months, as our teamwork had developed and become more and more instinctive, he'd developed a bit of a cocky streak. Nothing fazed him at all. He'd add little flourishes to his tasks, the kind of extra that in football they would call 'showboating' – a flick of a paw here, a well-timed yap there, a wink and a smile. If he could have spoken when answering the phone he'd have said, 'Speak to my publicist!' The guy/dog was a born entertainer. Unlike his master, who just so happened to be me. When other people were watching us, I simply wanted to get it over and done with. My heart would be pounding, my entire body sweating. In fact, thinking about it, I wasn't a million miles away from the state I was in when I angrily welcomed Lian into my life that shameful morning. Only this feeling wasn't quite so intense and berserk.

With one week until the big show I was a bag of nerves, and Canine Partners had taken on the look of a torture chamber.

'So how are you feeling about the big show coming up?' asked Nina softly. It was a kind question, well meant, and it was probably supposed to signal the beginning of a calmly spoken conversation about how I was feeling confident, and I was looking forward to it.

Instead, I started shaking visibly, and pleading desperately with my eyes for her to change the subject. How could she be so casual? Just throwing questions like that at me from nowhere? Was she taunting me?

'Honestly?' I said. 'Honestly, I wish the show bit wasn't happening.'

'But you two are fantastic!' she cooed, smiling widely.

'It's not that, I know we can do this. It's more the, um, people.'

'Oh, don't worry about them.' She chuckled. 'You'll be perfect, Liam, you just need to believe in yourself. Aero thinks you're great.'

I looked down to my dog, mooching around at the end of my leash. He was nodding up at me, as if to confirm that, yep, it's true, he thought I was great. He knew we were a dynamite team. I so wished that I could have his confidence.

I glanced around the Canine Partners grounds, and saw the other four terrible teens scattered in different areas of the field, all enjoying a private moment with their dogs. The enormity of all this hit me, and I wondered if it had dawned on them as well. Just a few short months ago we were standing in this exact same field, all grimacing as Nina talked us through what we were going to be doing. Not one of us seemed happy to be there, and when confronted by the dogs we all shifted around awkwardly, having no idea what to do with these strange drooling creatures.

The transformation had been huge. Each pair had bonded, and if I listened closely I could hear the murmur of everyone talking softly to their pups, encouraging them, not just playing the part of dog trainer, but playing the part of friend as well. It was amazing, and made for quite a picture. No one passing by would think that there was a field of troubled kids who could barely cope at school and were probably moments away from

total exclusion just a few months ago; now we looked like dili-
gent young adults. Again, as usual, my chest puffed out with
pride, making me look like a strange lanky human peacock.
I wasn't proud only of myself and Aero either, I was proud
of us all. In my estimation, Rob, Ellie, Allie and I must have
looked like lost causes on that first day. Here was the proof that
we were worth persevering with. Shy Katrina had positively
blossomed.

'I never thought I was a bad kid,' said Rob that lunchtime.
'I've always thought I was pretty decent; it's the rest of the world
that can't stand me.'

Everyone laughed, Nina included. We'd come a long way
together as a group and we were tight; even the grown-ups
working there liked having us around. I know that for a fact,
because at least three of them told me so. Their exact words
were: 'It's going to be weird when you kids go.' That's proof
enough for me!

We all prepared for the show differently. Rob was totally
at ease with performing in front of people. In fact, if he could
have an appreciative audience follow him around in his day-
to-day life he would. They probably wouldn't even have to be
that appreciative. Just an audience. He was excited about the
show, as were Ellie and Allie. They were all far more comfortable with attention than Katrina and me. I think I was by
far the most uncomfortable with it; a few weeks previously
Katrina had plucked up the courage to do a talk in front of a
classroom full of kids, and since then she was like a different
girl. I heaped more and more pressure on myself, worried that
my performance anxiety would ruin everything for Aero. I
couldn't do that.

In the week running up to the show my mind went through
every possible bad outcome. I had nightmares about falling off
the stage and landing in a lump with a spinning wheelchair
next to me on the floor, as the audience looked on shaking their
heads or laughing hysterically. I imagined opening my mouth

and being unable to speak. I wondered what would happen if I suddenly projectile-vomited into the front row. What if I started giggling nervously? I asked myself. Oh, God, what if I get totally bogged down beneath the world's most horrific blushing fit?

These were cruel mind tricks that I needed to escape from. Unfortunately, I couldn't. I'd go to the park with Lian, and all I could think about was the show. Mum would be talking to me about where we should go on holiday this year, and all I could see was a hundred sets of eyes trained on me, waiting for me to fall flat on my face. If I overheard a dog barking in the distance, I would suddenly think about Aero turning nasty in the middle of the show and attacking me, and rather than dutifully collecting up bits of washing from the machine, he'd leap fifty feet into the air and land on my lap, then sink his teeth into my jugular, and finish off the whole performance with some kind of cheeky flourish. Yes, some might argue that I was over-thinking matters a touch. But this journey had been so brilliant for me that I didn't want it all to go wrong right at the last hurdle. Unfortunately, I knew that the more I wound myself up and worried about it, the more likely it would be to turn into a disaster.

The big day hurtled my way at breakneck speed, and before I could catch my breath it was upon us. I did notice that while the other days zipped past, once the actual day of the show came, time decided to stand still. Every minute took two minutes, every hour felt like a day in itself. All I wanted was to be on that stage enjoying the adulation, but the more I stared at my watch, the less inclined it seemed to be to tick, let alone tock. And I hadn't even finished breakfast yet.

'You all set for the show, Liam?' Mathew beamed later as I clambered into the family car – destination, school – my legs shaking like I was made of spaghetti. Every part of me was motoring. Or was that just the motor?

'To answer your question, Mathew – no, no, I'm not ready, would you be ready?'

My brother did that thing where you blow on your fingernails and rub them on your chest. It meant yes, he would be ready, but what that gesture signifed to me is, 'I really don't have a clue.'

'I'm terrified!' I shrieked, looking at Mum.

'Of course you are, darling, it's a challenge.'

'Thank you!' I exclaimed. 'At least someone else is a human being.'

'It's good to be nervous, shows you're human.' She smiled.

'Not my fault if you can't take the pressure,' chirped Mathew, loving taking the mickey.

The car was so tense, you could almost smell the adrenaline. Or, at least, I'm pretty sure that's what it was. I started mumbling through my bit.

'. . . blah, blah, GOOD BOY, blah, blah, DOOR, blah, blah . . .'

'You all right there, son?' boomed Dad, looking into the rear-view mirror, his eyes full of sympathy.

'I'm looking forward to it actually,' I honked, smiling like a maniac. I couldn't have been more fake if I'd been reading the words from an autocue.

I burst into tears.

'Oh, who am I kidding, I'm petrified!'

This was shaping up to be the weirdest car journey the family had ever endured, which was really saying something.

'I'm sorry, Liam, I didn't mean to upset you,' muttered Mathew, totally confused, 'just, you know, joking.'

'I'll be fine,' I spluttered.

We sat in silence as the car pootled down country lane after bigger road after country lane.

I was staring blankly out of the window, and if I'm not entirely mistaken, there were beads of sweat forming around my temples.

'Stop the car!' shouted Mathew. 'I know what we should do.' He looked at me and nodded, like this was a great idea.

'Dad, can we stop?' I asked in a calm voice.

'We're almost there,' said Dad.

'Dad, you're a good man,' I noted, 'but I really think we should stop.'

The car pulled over next to one of the nearby rolling green fields.

'We can't be long, kids,' said Dad in a stern voice, 'we're on a schedule. Does someone need a wee?'

'Right, everyone,' said Mathew, clapping his hands together. 'What I suggest is that we all head into that field and scream at the top of our voices – it's called primal screaming, and it's a great way to get rid of tension. Liam, it will do you the world of good, and as a family I think we should all support him. Mum? Sophie?'

I raised my eyebrow, and looked at the girls. They shrugged; it sounded like a perfectly good idea to them.

And thus the four of us skipped over the small stone wall, and headed towards the centre of the field. It only felt rebellious because we really should have been on the way to school.

'We'll be literally one minute, Dad,' said Mathew, doing a thumbs up.

Dad didn't look overly bothered, he was happy enough. We hadn't thought to invite him to join us, because, believe me, he'd have said no. Primal screaming wasn't really his thing.

'Right, after three, everyone, just let it all out,' declared Mathew.

'Let what out?'

'All the tension, scream it all out at the top of your voice. No one will hear us, we're in the middle of nowhere.'

'That's true.' I nodded.

'Right…ONE…TWO…THREE!ARRRRRGGGGGG HHHHHHHHHHHH!'

I looked to the heavens, bellowing my guts out. It felt great, as if my insides might shoot from my mouth in flames. After about thirty seconds I was out of puff, and stopped. I was done.

'. . . EEEEEEEEEEEEEEEEEEEUUUUUUUUUUURR RRRGGGGHHHHH!'

And that was Mum done. Something told me that she'd just banished a few years of pent-up anger and frustration with a certain little boy. We caught our breath, and bounced back to the car, all feeling as light as a feather.

'Nice thinking, matey!' I said, putting my arm around Mathew's shoulders.

'You lot finished shouting in fields now?' deadpanned Dad, as we trundled off in the direction of our destiny.

By the time we got to school, everyone was in good spirits. I caught up with the others. Rob, of course, was cracking jokes, and all the girls had gone that extra mile to do themselves up – they were in their best outfits, with classy make-up. I'd followed all Lian's handy exfoliating tips, and did feel fresh. She'd recommended that I use conditioner as well as shampoo on my hair, so I'd snaffled some of Mum's and I was slightly concerned that my hair smelled womanly. Aero had a sniff, and didn't seem too offended by it.

As expected, I'd spent most of the afternoon attempting to make Aero look presentable, which was a job akin to making a drifter look like a bank manager. I'd done my best: we'd spent an astonishing amount of time in the doggy shower, with me scrubbing soap and shampoo into his coat with the same grace and good technique as a decent sheep shearer. Once he'd dried off by soaking absolutely everything and everyone around him, I'd got busy with brushing his coat. I checked his teeth, eyes and nose to make sure he looked dazzling and healthy. And then off we went for a mid-afternoon jog around the field. I had some nervous tension to get rid of, plus Aero had some tremendous grooming work to undo. Within seconds he looked like he'd tangled with a particularly spiky hedge – the bank manager had morphed back into the drifter. Oh well.

Then, like a black hole that could bend space, time and probably something else, it was time for our graduation show.

'Guys, good luck tonight!' boomed Rob like a stage school maniac or a deranged aerobics instructor, striding around backstage.

'What is *with* you today?' I asked. 'Are you on drugs?'

'No, just keeping moving,' he said. 'Getting that adrenaline pumping before the performance, maintaining decent blood pressure, keeping those butterflies in the cage, um . . . yeah.'

Rob marched into the centre of the room with his arms outstretched like a teenage Christ – was this from *Billy Elliot* or something? I thought.

'I'm meditating,' he informed me with a dramatic wink. This was like a strange dream, and everyone was making me even more nervous. Stage fright can make people a little odd, I concluded.

'What about the dogs?' I said. 'Do they need to meditate?'

'Joke all you like, Liam,' huffed Rob, getting rather impatient. 'I'm just putting into practice what I know.'

I apologized with a firm pat on the back. 'Sorry, buddy, I'm a bit scared, I'm not used to this kind of thing.'

'You'll be excellent, mate, don't you realize that you're top of the class? You and Aero are the ones to beat!'

Top of the class? Needless to say, no, I hadn't figured that out, and it most certainly wasn't a spot in the class that I was accustomed to. The thought of it made me beam, a broad grin spreading right across my face. Of course, now would be the perfect time to be caught on camera, but, as had been the case for the last few months, the film makers appeared to be on a tea and sandwich break whenever anything amazing happened to me.

'Thanks, Rob,' I gushed, before giving him a strange handshake/hug combo that didn't really work. It was well meant, but Rob didn't seem overly comfortable with it, and, honestly, why would he? I was notorious for lurching forward to hurt people, not hug them.

But I was a changed man. We had been on such a wonderful journey together, us kids, one that no one else would really understand. The TV show would capture the images of us on that first day, the first throes of the training, the trials and tribulations. But it wouldn't pick up on the tense vibes on that bus when we first started out, or the confusion and insecurity we all felt away from our natural habitat, our comfort zones. This course had stripped us down and built us back up again. In hindsight, it was probably for the best that the cameras couldn't pick up the nervous backstage tension we were going through – I don't think I could relive the anxiety. It was horrid.

'Okay, guys, let's do this, let's go out there and show those people that we are professionals,' barked Rob, back in the land of the living.

We all instinctively cheered and whooped a bit. And then I returned to my anxious thoughts.

'It's almost show time, people!' enthused Nina, clapping her hands, and everything I'd been nervously waiting for began.

I tentatively peeked out at the stage.

I reached into my pocket for a doggy treat, sensing Aero's excited breath on my hand. He chomped it with his usual gusto, looking at me with an inquisitive cock of the head. His furry ears, a darker shade of blond than the rest of him, were at a wonky angle and gave him a slightly comical look. The hours spent vigorously combing his coat really had been totally wasted, I thought with a grin. I imagined I was seeing him for the first time, and he looked hilarious.

He demonstrated a similar line in looking scruffy that I've been delicately honing for years. Even in the world's most amazing designer suit I'd look like I'd just run naked through a jumble sale to get dressed. It's quite a skill. One that Aero and I shared, it seemed. As I bent down to stroke him, his fur smelled of woody adventures and he looked like he'd tried to smooth himself down after a fight with a bush and a few elusive squirrels.

Still, I couldn't help but forgive Aero his appearance. He might not look like he'd had a wash and blow dry or a manicure, but in some ways I now knew that I owed that dog my life. In those moments backstage awaiting our destiny, the last few months seemed to flash before my very eyes, a bit like I expect it works when people insist that they saw their whole lives flash in front of them during a near-death experience. Thankfully, there wasn't much chance of dying on this occasion. Except on stage, of course.

'He needs to learn boundaries – how to be polite and respectful around other people.' That was what Nina told me before I met him. Funny that. It was exactly the same as teachers and various other grown-ups had been saying – well, shouting – about me for years.

The difference was, when we first met, Aero was a cute fourteen-month-old puppy who didn't know any better. I was fifteen and I still hadn't mastered not being a complete pain in the bum. In those months of training and bonding, and embarking on the greatest adventure of my life, we'd moved closer to fulfilling our potential, and this show was the culmination of that. Aero, the pup, had morphed into a grown-up dog, and Liam, the turdy little oik, was very nearly a polite young gentleman.

Of course, Aero had always been mostly polite, and would never swear, or at least not when I was listening. But when things weren't going his way, some of his growls and woofs would take on a bit of a gobby tone. Like he was doing the doggy equivalent of me embarking on one of my colourful four-letter-worded steams that had become so notorious at my school. But, slightly ridiculously, it was my job to put him straight. To let him know that he needed to behave – and how to do it. It could have been a case of the blind leading the blind, yet weirdly it was almost the other way round. I had trained Aero, but in some more subtle ways he had also trained me. We were both scruffy pups, but we were looking out for each other. Standing there, drinking in the atmosphere, that's how it felt anyway. Aero was showcasing what he could do given a few intensive months with a troubled teenager, while I was showing off my doggy training skills.

Which is what brings us back to the stark white hall, about to perform a demonstration of just how well behaved and brilliant Aero could be – not to mention how far his anxious trainer had come in the last few months.

We'd spent the last three months building up to this moment. Even though my confidence had come along in leaps and bounds, I still couldn't believe how nervous I was. It was worse than talking to girls – even worse than that fateful morning a few weeks ago when I'd met Lian. By now, my legs were tired and shaking, my heart was thumping, lodged somewhere in my throat. That my mouth was completely dry was a worry, and the chances of words actually coming out if I wanted to speak seemed hugely unlikely.

The crowds were piling into the hall, making the usual din. All the teenagers allowed to attend were doing their level best to freak me out even more by shrieking, screaming, running around, and generally acting crazy. It could easily have been a day at school. Normally, I'd be the one making the most noise. They were making their presence felt.

In my case, I'd only ever been noisy and irritating because I didn't fit in. I was just the weird, lanky loner with the straggly brown fringe over my eyes, hiding a scowl, wearing a tie with such a minuscule knot in it that even a needle-fingered robot would struggle to unravel it – it had been my vibe, and it was a look I'm pretty sure I'd stolen from an episode of *Grange Hill*. People had laughed along with me, some kids had been too terrified of me to tell me I'd be wiser to shut the heck up. Being loud and aggressive had been my way of coping with the strange hand that life had dealt me. Better to get noticed than to fade to grey somewhere on the back row, with all the other geeks and nerds who didn't belong – that's what I'd thought anyway. And yet, here I was, about to show these people my 'sensitive side'. It felt really peculiar, and I was worried that once the spotlight

hit my face I'd morph into the angry young moron I was trying
to make everyone forget about.

I looked at my dog. Aero had been the first person (okay, I
know he's not strictly *a person)* who didn't make me feel like an
eccentric outsider. From the minute I saw him I'd known that
he was the dog version of me – hyperactive, with an attitude,
but deep down basically brilliant and lovely(!), someone who
wanted to learn the ropes and stay out of trouble. We bonded
instantly. When I had a strop, or couldn't cope, he hadn't looked
at me as if I were scum. His liquid brown eyes just looked ques-
tioning. Like he was asking, 'What's up?' Not judging me as
an antisocial loser with stupid hair – not that I have stupid hair
of course, just using it as an example. Maybe it was simply that
he couldn't talk and tell me to get lost. But whatever it was, it
worked. In those first days of knowing him, I can honestly say
it was the first time I'd got out of bed in the morning actually
looking forward to the day ahead. Might sound a bit harsh, but
it's true. Before all this, getting up to face the day had been
difficult. Not only for me either – Mum, Mr Blackmore, all my
other teachers had felt the effects of Liam Creed, awoken and
spreading his trail of destruction.

But in the silence of those green Canine Partners fields,
with cloudy skies overhead and a young dog who couldn't say
anything more significant than 'yap' to me, I felt like life was
finally making sense. Dramatic as that sounds.

Even so, that felt a long way from where I was now. Over
the noise of the crowd I could just about make out Mum's voice
soaring above the rest – she is not, as you well know by now,
a quiet woman. With a son like me, that's a good thing. But it
gave my nerves another kick in the groin. To say I'd put Mum
through a lot would be the understatement of the century. I
wanted her to be proud of me, *she* wanted to be proud of me,
and now was the perfect time to do it. Which was a bit more
pressure than someone like me could usually manage to take.
But weirdly I couldn't feel that buzzing of bad electricity start

to swirl round my head. The one that switched on swear-words, strops and surly behaviour. It had always been like a short circuit in my brain. This going on the straight and narrow experiment might just have worked, I decided.

Making people proud of me had never been my strong point. Until now.

The grumpy, rude scruffbag who had first met Aero had been replaced by a happy, well-adjusted scruffbag (well, you can't have everything. Not even the new me could be *that* perfect. It wouldn't be fair to everyone else).

'You ready for this, Liam?' said Mr Blackmore, patting me supportively on the back. He had given me my lucky break, and I really wanted him to feel that it was worth the gamble. His eyes were crinkled up in a smile, looking directly at me. Oddly, he was looking like this was a proud moment for him too. It made me nervous. I wasn't used to this, it was a whole new ball game. For the first time I felt like I had something to lose, beyond my place at school and my pocket money. I finally had a purpose, and I so wanted to show everyone how amazing Aero and I could be.

'Yeah,' I grunted back with all the finesse of a sullen teenager. I might have been pulling my socks up, but being a whizz with words was still in the amoeba stage of my evolution. But the happy twinkle in my eyes spoke louder than words. I'd finally found something I was good at. It was actually quite strange to have a teacher look at me without an expression of absolute despair. It really was making me feel quite odd. I realized how much easier it was to say eff off than something nice, like thank you. And if anyone needed to be on the receiving end of a bit of my gratitude it was Mr Blackmore.

He was up there on my list of people I owed a lot to. I'd spent quite some time working on this list. Mum was at the top, she'll be pleased to find out (other than the times she won't let me watch Sky, then she gets struck off until I'm in a better mood). There have been moments when Aero's topped the list ahead of her, but I thought that was a bit mean considering she did that whole giving birth to me and bringing me up business. Not an easy task. So to spare everyone's blushes I've got a list for humans and a list for dogs. Aero's top of the dogs, which makes him happy. And Mum's my number one two-legged creature. But Mr Blackmore comes a close second (to Mum, that is; he didn't have four legs and respond to the word 'fetch' last time I checked). Like Mum and Aero, he had believed in me when no one else would. Without him, I wouldn't be here, sweaty-palmed, with a young dog by my side. Desperate for the toilet.

'Don't worry, I know you won't let everyone down,' he told me confidently, sensing my nerves, which were chugging faster, and faster, like an out-of-control oncoming train. His blue tie was knotted really tight like mine, and I focused on that before looking him in the eyes. Now I knew it was okay to be scared. I wasn't ashamed any more. We had the same tie style. Perhaps in a former life Mr Blackmore had been a little bit like me? Might that have been why he appeared to have so much faith in me?

It made me think back to that fateful day when he'd told me the news. He'd called me into his office, which I automatically thought meant I was about to get it in the neck. But instead he had announced that he was putting me forward to take part in a TV show where disobedient teenagers train dogs to behave. Of course, me being me, my first question had been something along the lines of 'Great, does that mean I get out of school?' He had let out quite a loud, exasperated sigh at that.

'Don't let us down, Liam,' he had told me, with none of the confidence he was speaking to me with today. Back then he'd looked very world-weary and unsure, like he didn't know if he was doing the right thing, but didn't have any better ideas up his sleeve. His whole body language had screamed, 'This is a big, massive gamble and I'm *scared*! Me! A teacher! Scared!' I knew I wasn't a safe bet. But now he looked like he was at the bookies about to collect his winnings.

'How are you doing, little fella?' Mr Blackmore bent down

to give Aero a stroke, his starched trousers creasing at the knees to get on eye level with him.

Aero gave him an excited yap in reply, pressing his wet nose into Mr Blackmore's hand affectionately. He could tell Mr B was one of the good guys. As I glanced at the exit, I was surprised that I wasn't tempted to bolt through it. In the past my thinking process used to go roughly like this: What does it matter if I bunk off? Everyone thinks I'm a failure, so if I mess this up it doesn't matter. People will just shrug and say, 'That's Liam for you,' like they always do. A loser has nothing to lose. Easy.

But that negative voice, the one that usually sat on my shoulder and squawked into my brain, was strangely quiet. I didn't miss it, that's for sure.

Seeing yourself grow up in such a short space of time is quite an odd experience. It's like accelerating from 0 to 100 in a Porsche, and leaving a hapless part of yourself behind on the hard shoulder. I could still see the bemused expression on the old me's face. He was probably giving me the two-fingered salute, bless him.

To prove that my transformation wasn't totally complete, just at that moment a pretty girl with shoulder-length strawberry hair came into view, staring at our little group, me standing with a teacher and a dog. I instantly turned beetroot red, as if I'd just been put in a pickle jar, then had the thermostat whacked up to nuclear. She had popped on a skirt that was shorter than is strictly legal, and if the rumours are true, most of the boys at school had been somewhat transfixed by this seriously fierce chick striding towards the main hall moments earlier, all legs and make-up. I looked down at my scuffed trainers, my fringe dangling in my eyes, hoping that by plastering as much hair over my face I didn't look in any way like I was perving.

I took a breath, and calmed the blushes, which thankfully (and miraculously) disappeared as she got closer. Mr Blackmore was blathering on, totally unaware of the fact that we were about to have company. I kept my cool.

'You've done really well, Liam. I knew you had it in you, you're a natural with dogs – especially Aero.'

I glanced down and saw Aero's tongue loll out, like he was agreeing with every word Mr Blackmore was saying.

Then I felt a pull at the leash, and saw – well, only just, through my fringe cum blindfold – the girl break into a massive, beaming smile as she approached us. Aero strained even harder on his leash, trying to scramble towards her.

'Heel, boy, heel,' I told him firmly, feeling proud that I was in some sort of control.

The girl's squeal carried right down the corridor. 'Oh, my God, he's *so* cute,' I heard her say.

Nice of you to say so – ha ha. Okay, obviously, she was talking about Aero – the skirt magnet by my side who was looking at her with puppy-dog eyes (well, not that he can help that, I suppose. After all, he is a puppy dog with eyes).

'Is he yours?' she asked, wrinkling up her nose to pull some sort of cute face at Aero. This, by the way, was a girl coming up to me and talking to me. And she wasn't Lian. This had never happened.

Mr Blackmore went to answer the question, but I got in there first. I was like a proud dad, I wanted to show off about my superdog.

'He's not mine, he belongs to—' I started off, wanting to launch into the full explanation. Hopefully, she had a few hours.

'Oh, is he yours then?' she asked, cutting me off before I could carry on with my ramblings, turning to face Mr Blackmore.

Aero was busy licking her hand, making a real meal of it. What a hero.

'No, he belongs here, to Canine Partners – the charity that trains dogs to assist disabled people,' the teacher informed her with a smile. 'But Liam's helping to train him.'

She turned back to look at me, with something that appeared to be admiration registering on her face. 'Really? You help train dogs? Ah, you're one of the stars of the show then?' she asked, sounding very impressed.

'Yes, I am. I've been training Aero – that's his name – and I'm really into it, it's really cool . . .' I was babbling. It's always the same. With girls I generally have only two gears: silently sullen, or motor-mouth babble. And the acceleration is pretty rapid. Since I'd hooked up with Lian and realized that girls are a complete puzzle, I tended to go for the babble rather than the mumble. Okay, so I wasn't Mr Smooth, but it was a big improvement.

Luckily, she wanted to know all about the cute little fella. And she was quite interested in what I had to say about Aero too . . .

'Is that his name? Aero? What a cute name!'

She gave him another cuddle, and Aero looked like he was enjoying it way too much. I tried to give him a filthy look, but he avoided my eye and nuzzled into her hand.

'How come he's called Aero?' she asked, looking at me curiously.

'I don't know,' I replied, the cogs of my brain whirring in a loud and confused manner. Weirdly, I'd never really thought about his name before. He'd just been Aero, no questions asked. Basically, he was named after a chocolate bar – simple.

But thinking on my feet, I managed to wheel out the pure cheese. 'He's like an Aero bar – bubbly and he'll make you melt.'

'That's funny!' She grinned, giving Aero an extra tickle just to prove he'd totally melted her.

Thinking about it, maybe he was the Brad Pitt of dogs. I wasn't doing too badly myself. Mr Blackmore looked over, stunned by my ability to crack a joke and talk to a girl. He'd seen the old me at school. He knew my furnace face.

'Anyway, shouldn't you be off to your seat before it starts?' Mr Blackmore asked the girl, as time was ticking by and I needed to get myself ready.

'Suppose so,' she replied, breaking off the love-in happening between her and Aero, which had reached frankly obscene levels.

I have never entirely figured out what this vision of legginess was doing backstage at a dog show: had Lian sent her to check up on me? Or was she a friend or relative of one of the other kids? Perhaps Katrina's over-confident sister?

It didn't really matter, I'd behaved myself. I was totally in love with Lian, and it suddenly occurred to me. I was hugely impressed by Aero's slick style with the women. Yes, I'd always been impressed by his confident manner around other dogs, but he even had an eye for a sexy lady. This dog was swiftly morphing into my GOD. This was definitely one area he could train me in. When you're getting relationship tips off a dog, it's a worry, I know – but, hey, so what? I've got problems.

'You're both good lads.' Mr Blackmore laughed, bending down to stroke Aero who was looking a bit forlorn at the loss of his new lady friend.

Seeing Aero and Mr Blackmore together, my two staunchest supporters, gave me a warm fuzzy feeling, a bit like my first can of lager had done.

For once, I hadn't let down the people who trusted in me.

I'd learned that there was more to life than mucking about, swearing and legging it when the pressure was on. I'd realized that it wasn't just about me, and what felt right in my camp – there were other people (and pooches) counting on me.

So, this is what growing up feels like, I thought, with something almost like awe. It was amazing how much I'd changed since that day in Mr Blackmore's office.

If someone had told me a few months ago that I'd be taking to the stage in front of my friends, family and dreaded teachers, I'd have assumed it was as some kind of example of how not to live your life, or they'd managed to pass a law introducing public hanging for tearaway teenagers – with a one-off permit especially for me.

And yet here I was, desperate to projectile-vomit into a bucket, sick with nerves. *Over a dog.* But still, I needed to do this, and, weirdly, I wanted to be there. I wanted to prove the doubters wrong. But more than anything I wanted to do it for the person who counted most: the one with a wet nose and four clumsy paws.

I looked over at Aero, who had missed his moment of inspirational hero completely, and was now attempting to torture and execute a poor spider who had stumbled across his path. That's my boy. He looked up and wagged his tail, then pounced on the spider again, waggling his head from side to side in a frenzy, his ears shaking madly.

It choked me up knowing that beneath his playful, mischievous behaviour (purely for my benefit, to calm my nerves, I'm sure) beat the heart of a well-behaved dog. With one command I could get him to sit, lie down or come to heel.

'Praise, rewards and positive reinforcement.' That had been Nina's mantra throughout. What a woman she had turned out to be – charismatic boss at the dog centre, all-round brilliant human being. She was a canine guru with thirty-five years' experience of moulding pooches into perfect dogs. When she told me this pearl of wisdom, in her strong Australian accent, her thick black eyebrows furrowed together to make the point of how important it was, something didn't make sense to me.

'What, so you don't tell them off if they've been bad?' I asked, confused by years of expertise in this whole behaving badly lark.

'Dogs learn by being praised for doing the right thing, not scolded for getting it wrong,' she had confirmed with an intense stare in my direction.

I certainly wished that my various doctors and medics and teachers had known about this technique when I was a small flower-rearranging nipper. 'Oh,' I had replied, slightly miffed, as I stewed it over in my mind. So dogs deserve the benefit of the doubt, but we kids don't, I had thought.

It was strange and funny looking back at all those early sessions with the dogs. I had spent most of them focused on my own plight, jealous of the great treatment the dogs got, even when they were up to no good. The entire planet prior to Canine Partners had been hurtling around me. I was the centre of the universe. I felt ashamed and embarrassed of the person I was then. But also happy with the person I was becoming. I'd love to say the person that I'd become, but there's still plenty of work to be done. Room for improvement.

It wasn't like I was angling for a doggy treat or anything, but as all the years of being hauled into the headmasters' office flashed before me, I just wished that someone had taken me to one side to say a few words of encouragement. More steel reinforcement than positive reinforcement there.

In his own way, Aero knew how to throw a few affirmations my way – even if it was only communicated with a wagging tail. With my heart hammering away merrily to a techno beat in my chest, Aero yapped at me with concern. It was his way of telling me to calm down, reassuring me that everything would be okay. I knew he could sense my anxiety. He'd been really playful all day, as if trying to distract me from the fact that I was about to face my biggest fear: being taken seriously. Well, okay, my second biggest fear behind being stuck in a lift with only a family of creepy clowns for company. I checked my mental clock – about three and a half minutes before facing my destiny.

'Thanks for taking a chance on me,' I told Mr Blackmore awkwardly, managing to meet his gaze.

He slapped his hand on my shoulder and said he was thrilled with how it had all worked out. He knew, and I knew, that I had become so much nicer to be around than the mouldy old Liam that everyone used to know and loathe.

It seemed slightly surreal that I, the person who had tried his hardest to be a rebel without a cause – or should I say paws! (sorry, I couldn't help myself) – was about to become the school swot, and was worrying like mad about making the grade. I walked towards the main backstage area, Aero trotting obedi-ently behind me. His ears bobbed up and down as he checked out every object we walked past, pulling on the lead as he tried to give everything a good once-over sniff. Sometimes, when he was really excited, his tail stood up on end, the little blond hairs fluttering with every quick little wag. He was doing that now. He sensed it was his big moment too.

'You ready now, Liam?' said Mr Blackmore, guiding us to the back of the stage.

The honest answer to that – no. I did a last checklist in my head. Butterflies: check. Dog: check. Astonishingly sweaty armpits: check. Chances of passing out: high.

Months of barking and disobedience (and that's only me), and this was it, just me and my dog – and nearly a hundred people watching closely to judge the pair of us. It was us against them.

People had obviously never really worked for me – far too complicated. Dogs, though, they'd turned out to be a whole different ball game. If they're happy, their joy is absolute. If they're angry, they bark a bit until it's all out. As far as I'm concerned, they're miles ahead of us humans on the social and evolutionary scale. I now knew why, when running around in a field with Aero, I'd never been more comfortable in my own skin. He understood me, I didn't need to explain myself or apologize ('sorry' is not the hardest word by around the ten thousandth time, Elton John). He didn't mock my clothes, my shoes, or my poorly attempted moustache – which I won't be trying again in a hurry, by the way. But there was something else, too. Another reason why the little guy and me had bonded so well. It's been playing on my mind for a while. Ever since I first saw Aero tear through a flower border, uprooting all the plants and innocently beheading all the pink flowers, I'd had this idea clunking around in my brain, which bears repeating: Puppies have ADHD too.

Before Susan and myself had started working with him, Aero hadn't known how to act around other people, and he didn't know what behaviour was acceptable and what would get him into a whole lot of trouble. So as a pup he'd spent a lot of time confused. Scratching his whiskers about why he was often in the bad books. Sometimes he had a whole heap of energy and just wanted to tear around. Sometimes he was bored and only wanted to flop in his doggy bed. His mind was whirring with a million thoughts of doggy biscuits, walks, stuff to chase, things to bite, flies to catch and spiders to tease. When he met someone, he didn't know if he should lick their hand or wee on their shoes. So sometimes he did both. Just to be safe.

He wanted to see the world, but sometimes it frightened him. Big trucks especially. When it all got too much for him, he wanted to hide – under the bed, in a shed, inside a big prickly bush, wherever would have him really.

He was not being sullen, he was simply scared.

If he rolled in mud then walked it into the carpet, he didn't mean to ruin it. He just didn't know any better. That's why he needed to be trained. But first, before he was shown the ropes, he needed someone to love him and believe in him.

Someone who knew he was a good dog who sometimes behaved badly.

'Okay, Liam and Aero – you're on!'

All my friends were backstage, and after a group hug, Nina had virtually to push me forward, with Aero yapping, his eyes blinking in the bright lights, by my side.

Confidently, we strode on to the stage together.

How had we ever made it this far?

It was a miracle, and I was grateful for it.

In my twisted imagination, I'd spent weeks recreating this moment – walking into a dark theatre with a dazzling spotlight glaring directly into my eyes, blinding me. A zillion faceless heads all peering at me in the shadows. The stage would be heavy and wooden, with gigantic draping red curtains at the sides, like the ones you see in old films. And of course, there would be a complete pin-dropping silence, everyone waiting for me to stumble and stutter and make a fool of myself. Oh, the drama! It was going to be horrendous.

The reality, however, wasn't anything like that.

I hadn't taken into account that I was going on stage with my best pal, so I was immediately comforted by that. And the actual layout of that main hall wasn't nearly so daunting. I could see all the faces in the crowd, lots of them were familiar to me, and, most importantly, they were all smiling at me, willing me to do well.

Talk about positive reinforcement.

As we emerged on to the stage, my whole relationship with my dog continued to flicker through my mind's eye. I remembered that first time we were left alone and I felt shy and self-conscious; then there was the time I couldn't even tug on his leash without freaking out, worried he might go for my jugular.

I saw all the frustrating attempts to shop, or to dress or to fetch the washing. The best bits flashed past too – the triumphs, the funny days running around in a field, the blossoming friendship.

No matter what happened in the next few minutes, it served as a reminder that nothing and no one could take away the great memories we had together.

'Ladies and gentlemen, introducing Liam and his dog, Aero!'

The applause woke me up, Aero yapped and I smiled and waved. The wheelchair was already on its spot, stage right, and the washing machine was wheeled on, placed around stage left.

'So, Liam, what will you and Aero be doing today?' Nina winked at me.

'Hello, Nina, great to be here.' I waved at the audience and heard Mum chuckling. 'Today I'm going to show you, with the aid of my pal Aero, how a Canine Partners dog can empty a washing machine better than any mum in the country.'

Again, the laughter rippled through the crowd, this time a little bit louder than before. It was a great feeling, this whole performing lark.

I boarded the wheelchair, and moved it into a comfortable position to face my dog. I couldn't resist the temptation to do a little wheelie that I'd mastered over the months – the crowd approved.

'Just a little wheelie there for you, ladies and gentlemen,' I boomed. 'It's a skill I've picked up along the way.'

A spattering of applause – it felt ace.

I called Aero over to me, his eyes fixed on mine, but he didn't move. What was going on?

'Come on, boy, don't let me down now,' I said, looking dramatically at the audience. In reality, my heart was about to tear through my top.

Had my pal frozen under the glare? Time slowed again as we stared at one another awkwardly, my eyes gesturing desperately for him to come over to me.

The auditorium went completely silent for all of three seconds – which, to me, felt like at least eight hours – and then . . . he bounded over.

'That's it, good dog!' I enthused. 'Good boy!'

The gallons of sweat waiting ready behind my skin called off the attack, as did the buckets of red blood travelling to my face to make me blush. I was suddenly caught in a grip of extreme calm.

'I am now, ladies and gentlemen, going to ask Aero to fetch my washing!' I cooed.

'Go on, Aero, fetch the washing!' I instructed.

And off he scurried in the direction of the washing machine, where he proceeded to open the door with his mouth – cue a sharp, impressed intake of breath from the audience.

'Oh, you ain't seen nothing yet!' I beamed.

A laugh. The door open, Aero went foraging for a laundry basket. It was to the right of the machine. He grabbed it in the front of his mouth and busily dragged it around to sit just beneath the door.

'That's it, Aero, good dog!'

Another 'ooh'– they were taking in the show of their life. Just wait until he starts unloading the washing, I thought. It's going to be awesome.

And so it was; he began removing the clothes and putting them in the basket like a tiny housewife covered in fur.

The audience made a silent hum of incredulity – the kind you might make if you couldn't quite believe your eyes. Was that really a dog emptying a washing machine?

They were definitely impressed by my clever furry buddy. With each item, they gasped louder and louder, and Aero unloaded with increasing vigour and gusto, now adding his little touches of flair, tossing underpants in the air, so they looped into the basket, adding socks to the pile with consummate ease.

Had there been a towel or two in there, he'd no doubt have started folding it into quarters, or wafting it about like a gymnast with a ribbon.

All the while I sat looking on as animated as possible, and enthusing 'Good Aero!', 'That's the stuff!' and, 'This, ladies and gentlemen, is a wonder-dog if ever there has been one!'

We were both milking the moment for all it was worth. I looked out into the audience. I could see Mum and Dad beaming at me, and Dad winked; Mr Blackmore looked impressed; Eileen, with Sailor by her side, looked mighty chuffed. Then, right at the back, obviously attempting to hide herself very badly, was Lian. She had snuck in to support me during my proudest moment, despite me telling her not to come. I was over the moon that she'd made it. Now I just needed to make sure that I didn't accidentally hurtle off the stage in my wheelchair, and this would officially become the finest day of my whole life.

'And now, ladies and gentlemen, Aero will help me undress!' I boomed. 'Although only partially, I'm afraid!'

More laughter, my ego further inflated. I popped on a cap for this one, doing so in a flashy way, a bit like when Michael Jackson puts on a trilby. Only with a less weird face.

'Come on, boy!' I honked dramatically, as Aero set about taking off my socks, biting at my feet with his teeth, but never once raising so much as a wince. This was a deft, exact science, and he was an expert.

He helped with the zip on my jacket, then, leaping into the air like a giant furry salmon, he snatched the peaked cap from my head in one slick movement. It was our crowning moment, the culmination of all the work we did, finished with a flourish.

Were this a Hollywood movie, the crowds would have bounced to their feet clapping and cheering like maniacs, and Lian would have rushed the stage, fallen into my arms, with Aero watching on like a cheeky R2D2 character. But this is real life. Instead the audience rose and gave us a civilized standing ovation – Mum whistled.

I threw down a handful of treats for my pal, and the biggest wave of happiness I've ever known washed over me. This was the high point of my life. As I looked around the room, all the most important people in my life were there: Mum, Dad, Nina, Lian, Eileen, Mr Blackmore. They were all smiling with delight, they all had tears in their eyes, they were all proud of me and my dog. I welled up too.

We took our bow and bounded backstage, the adrenaline still rushing around my body.

The others were all there, and we were all jumping up and down, the dogs yapping with excitement.

'That's was excellent!' enthused Rob, before dashing on to the stage for his turn.

He was right.

I decided to go and find Lian.

10

The TV show comes to an end

With the afterglow of our big moment wearing off, the reality of our mission really hit me. Our journey together was coming to an end. While I knew I was going to miss my dog more than anything, this was what we had been working towards – going our separate ways. Him out into a brand-new home and world where he could put his skills into practice and no doubt learn a few new ones along the way. I was going to miss being the one he looked to for new tricks or information, but I knew he'd make someone else as proud as he'd made me. And, well, I was going to be heading out into the big wide world a new man, one who had already managed a huge achievement. I had felt that burst of pride and energy that comes from doing something decent, not to mention something I was good at, and I wanted that buzz to continue.

I paid Nina a visit. She was standing quietly by the field, looking into the distance, enjoying a nice cup of tea.

'Hi, Nina,' I said in a slightly deeper growl than intended.

'Ah, hi, Liam, how's it going?'

I could speak easily to Nina now, and I wasn't ashamed or embarrassed to tell her that I was anxious about saying goodbye to my pal.

'Um, I'm a bit worried about Aero. He will be all right, won't he?'

'We'll keep track of him, Liam, and you'll always know that he's out there somewhere making someone who needs help happier and more independent than they could have imagined.'

I smiled. I knew she was right – working at Canine Partners for even a short while had opened my eyes to the reality of it. These carers were strong. The puppy parents might have looked like a sugary sweet sewing circle, but they would never lose sight of the fact that one day they would have to hand their little pup over to one of the trainers, and be done with it, until the next one. Our job was to be caring and loving, but also selfless enough to know when to let go of that love. That was a pretty big lesson to learn, I must say.

'Thanks, Nina, I know you're right.'

'You've done really well, Liam.'

'I know,' I agreed, a little bit arrogantly.

I wandered off to find my dog, my friend, my furry little mirror. It wasn't just me who had changed dramatically and excelled in the last few weeks. Aero had become an adult too. He could now quietly laze around in the vicinity of other dogs without vying for attention, and either my eyes were completely deluding me, or he had even started to look a little bit dapper. Obviously, he'd only developed this elegant demeanour since the big show, but still, he looked dapper none the less.

I was proud of him – and myself.

Everything about Canine Partners became meaningful in those last few days. I'd been going to the same place for months, it was so familiar, and yet the longer the course wore on, the more I understood our environment. Thinking back to those first experiences around the place, it must have looked so surreal and out of this world. I'd seen or imagined dog homes in the past, and I'd conjured up images of packed kennels, noisy with yapping dogs, and stern people stomping around with an air of authority, telling the furry folk what to do in loud, aggressive voices.

To me, it quickly became the nicest place in the world to be, because, come on, who can't be in a good mood when there are loads of cool dogs around?

Those furry little buggers are the best!

From the office, I'd stride down the stairs and into the hall-way, and, littered throughout the building, in every training room, in the kitchen, in the shower room, in the kennels, even upstairs in the swanky offices near the quiet business dogs, there were A4 sheets on the wall listing the commands to use on the pups, or giving crucial bits of information about how to keep your furry friend on the straight and narrow. Some laminated, some naked. We were there to do vital training, and those pieces of paper were an aid to keep everyone focused on the bigger picture, and remind us what was important. And thank goodness, or else we'd all be out in one of the fields scurrying around with our dogs, simply basking in the sunshine. I would have been anyway.

Lining the walls from the front entrance and all the way up to the offices, past the toilets, and stopping just in front of the little tea kitchen was the hall of fame celebrating all the top Canine Partners graduates – nicely framed pictures of previous Canine Partners dogs and their new owners, always smiling, their sense of relief and new-found independence caught perfectly on camera. Knowing that Aero would be on the wall one day very soon felt brilliant. I did wonder, though, if I'd feel jealous seeing him with a new, cheerful owner. I'd miss the little terror.

During lunch, everyone seemed a bit subdued.

'So, it's going to be strange not doing this any more,' under-stated Rob, enthusiastically biting into his sandwich. 'I mean, at first, I was totally not into it, but it's been wicked, and I loved the show the other night, that was a good laugh . . .' And he was off.

I sat listening, agreeing with just about every word he said, but not daring to try to slip a word of my own in edgeways. I learned long ago not to bother with that.

'We'll still be pals though, right?' he continued, looking at me with complete sincerity.

'Of course, good mates for life,' and we high-fived. I'd decided to allow the high five back into our repertoire of greetings, just as a bit of fun, after trying to avoid them for a while. Anyway, we'd actually got pretty good at them – there was none of that accidentally thudding the side of each other's hands, there was always a crisp, booming slap. The perfect high five, many would argue. It's genuinely difficult to find your perfect high-five partner, and by accident rather than design fate had intervened and found me mine. Over the course of the training, Rob and I had become pretty tight, and not just because of our talent for hand slapping. He was much louder than me, but we kind of balanced each other out. His mum has since commented that he seems quite calm when I'm around, and there's something about his total fearlessness that makes me not feel so self-conscious when I'm with him. If you put us in a massive witches' cauldron and mixed us up, you might just about scrape together one normal human being.

I'd made a lot of pals.

I'd even miss the girls. I'd never admit it to them, but they'd helped me with my confidence. I'd never have thought I could actually have a conversation with a girl without erupting into sweating confusion before I met Ellie and Allie. Of course, I still found them absolutely terrifying – they were tough cookies.

'So how's it going with that girlfriend of yours?' cooed Ellie.

'Yeah, what? Not bad . . . What?' I giggled.

'What's her name?'

'Er, Lian.'

'Arrgghh, he's making it up!' they all guffawed. 'What an idiot!'

Yep, I was going to miss those girls, all right.

I walked down to the kennels, sloped in to see Aero. He put his paws on the cage as I walked over to him. Every moment we had together now felt precious, and every single gesture seemed somehow to have more meaning connected to it.

'Hey, Liam, old buddy, don't ever leave me!' he was practically screaming out every time we saw each other. I knew he could understand what was going on; our performance in the hall had been the great crescendo we were all hoping for, and now we were reducing the pressure. I wasn't striding in nervously to see him and demanding that he go through the same routine over and over and over again until we knew it instinctively. Instead, we were winding down together, practising his skills more for old times' sake than anything else. He was ready to move on, and just seeing how he had grown made me want to cry whenever I thought about it. This must be how a proud parent feels, I thought. I must describe the feeling to Mum and Dad! It was excellent.

I knelt down for a wrestle, and Aero yapped and played as we scruffed each other up. I tagged on a leash, picked up my Frisbee and marched with a determined air towards the field. Official Canine Partners training might have come to an end – we could empty washing machines, call lifts, open doors, we could even trigger an alarm should a Canine Partners owner fall from their wheelchair – but now I wanted him to do some standard flashy dog stuff. I wanted him to catch a Frisbee in his teeth. I wanted people to witness my pal flying through the air like a doggy Superman, hurtling in slow motion towards an unidentified yellow object, then plucking it from the sky, thus making us both look supercool. Man and dog at their most sexy and brilliant.

I'd studied for this moment for all of about two weeks by taking a Frisbee to the park with my dad and brother. I knew that to make it work I'd need to be able to throw the thing properly, and on my first few attempts I probably looked like a chimp hurling a plate out of a cage, the toy fizzing off in random directions, most often crashing on to the grass in split seconds and rolling round and round in little circles before flumping down in a pathetic anticlimax. Thankfully, Dad was some kind of Frisbee champion or something. The man was a marvel.

'Don't try so hard, you need to throw it casually with a little flick of the wrist.' And with that, he'd flick the Frisbee for miles like a UFO going into orbit, making it float effortlessly to my brother. It looked seriously brilliant.

Prior to Canine Partners and Aero I'd have given up my Frisbee training after the first couple of goes, I was that appalling. But I stuck to it, taking my inspiration from my woofing pal who had never tired of practising difficult tasks until he mastered them, and by around midnight I was zipping my Frisbee past the silvery outline of the moon like a professional. I'm pretty sure it happened like that anyway.

So, by the time we were in the field to learn this cool new trick, I could dictate the speed, height and trajectory of my yellow flying toy. How could this ever go wrong? Aero would instinctively know what I was doing – we had a bond, for heaven's sake. Or, as actually happened, he'd have no idea whatsoever what I was trying to make him do. The first chuck he pretty much ignored, the second he waited for the Frisbee to land before charging off to pick it up like he would a tennis ball. The third somehow hit him in the face.

'Oh, come on, Aero, leap into the air and catch it!' I shouted, throwing it again. It was ideal, floating through the air, it just needed a salmon-like jump from my dog and we could travel the country as a novelty act and make it on one of those adverts in which dogs do that kind of thing. But no, again he waited for it to land, bounded after the toy and fetched it. He dropped it at my feet, looking up cheerfully. I realized that training was probably over, and, anyway, who cares if he can't strut across a field casually plucking Frisbees from the sky? My dog could still do unbelievable things, like run a household single-handed. This was unimportant. I took a tennis ball and launched it into the air; he understood the ball, we knew this game – and we were great at it.

As he hurtled after the ball, tracing its every bounce and change of direction before biting at it like a professional, I had a

sudden moment of clarity. For that second I was his new owner
in a wheelchair chucking a ball for my new pal to fetch. I could
see what he was going to see – an enthusiastic, cheerful dog who
loved to play in the park. A dog who could bring a smile to the
straightest of faces. I imagined how blessed his new owner was
going to feel as they zipped around the supermarket with their
trusted Aero at their side, helping to fetch tins, allowing passing children to stroke him. I saw the look of awe on their face
the first time they witnessed Aero busily emptying the washing
machine and piling the clothes expertly into a laundry basket.
I saw him calling lifts, answering the door, bouncing up to
remove a cap. But above and beyond any of that, I saw the look
of absolute contentment on their face as Aero curled up on the
floor enjoying a snooze after a long day. The glint in their eye
as a result of finally not having to struggle with their problems
alone every single minute of every single day. My dog was my
pal and my joy, but from now on he was going to be someone
else's lifeline. Tears flowed down my cheeks as he trotted back
to me with the grubby ball held proudly between his teeth.

I gave him the world's biggest ever hug.

'It's almost time to say goodbye, matey,' I cried.

I looked at him right in the eye; he stared back, sympathy and
kindness all over his face. He didn't like seeing me upset,
and he responded in the best way he could think of – by lurching forward, knocking me backwards and covering me in a
series of rancid doggy licks. I started laughing and pushed him
off me, as the pair of us wrestled in the middle of the field.

One more go, I decided, as we gathered ourselves together
and geared up to make it back to the kennel. I took the Frisbee and threw it into orbit. If this were a film, this would be
the moment, the one everyone had been waiting for. It had
been set up so perfectly: we'd had the failed montage of Frisbee
throws gone wrong, the emotional tears streaming down my
face, the laughter. This would surely be the icing on the cake
before the credits rolled and the audience sprang to their feet in

rapturous, tearful applause. As Aero flew through the air, with the gentle afternoon breeze ruffling his yellow coat, I would be filmed in the background desperately willing him on with my eyes, and when the significant catch was caught on freeze-frame, everything would slot into place. It would be a metaphor for how far we had come in this crazy journey of ours. But yeah, no luck, I'm afraid. The round yellow Frisbee looped on to the grass, and off he trundled after it. Oh well.

As we made our way back to the main hall, I decided to be brave and ask Nina some difficult questions. I'd been trying to avoid asking about the future.

'So where's he's going to go?' I asked Nina, making a poor attempt to hide the fact that it was completely ripping me to shreds on the inside.

'He's heading up north, Liam, to a man who really needs him, where everything you have taught him to do will come in mega-handy.'

The north, eh? I'd never really been up to that part of the world, but I'd always assumed that it rained a lot, and women in flowery dresses spent the whole day scrubbing their front steps with massive scrubbing brushes and overflowing tin buckets of water. Aero would get bored.

'I'm not sure he'll like the rain,' I confided in a whisper. 'I think somewhere sunny like Brighton would be far more suitable, don't you?'

Nina looked at me and smiled. 'This is just part of the job, Liam, and it's good that you're sad about it, it shows that you really care – that's a sign of a good dog trainer.'

'He'll be all right, won't he?' I said, tears welling in my eyes once again. Honestly, I'd probably spent fifteen years barely crying at all, but now it was almost every day, and it wasn't even sad crying. I just felt so emotional.

'You've got to stop asking me that, he'll be better than all right, Liam, he'll be great!' enthused Nina.

I knew she was right. I couldn't entirely work out what it was that was making me so sad – that I'd miss hanging around with him, or that I was worried that he'd forget me.

'He'll never forget the hard work you two have done together and he'll never forget you,' concluded Nina, obviously reading my mind without me realizing. How did she do that?

I felt better, but still nothing could prepare me for our final day at Canine Partners.

11

Bidding a fond farewell to Aero

The minibus stopped outside the house for the last time. I could hear the growling of the engine, and if I closed my eyes and listened hard enough I could make out Rob doing one of his monologues; recently these had taken the form of explaining a new dance move that he wanted to teach Ellie. She'd pretend not to be remotely interested, but on more than one occasion I'd caught her practising in the Canine Partners hall. I dragged myself together, heaping some styling gel into my hands and scraping my hair to one side. I zipped a razor over my top lip to catch any stray hairs bidding for escape – I had become an expert at doing this without cutting myself (often).

I lolloped downstairs to where Mum was sitting in the kitchen enjoying a big hunk of toast and jam. I grabbed half and scoffed it.

'Oi, thief!'

'I'll be off then, Ma!'

She stood up, came over and gave me a huge hug. 'You going to be all right?'

'Of course, he's just a stupid dog.'

'Don't be silly, Liam, he's much more than that and you know it.'

'I know. I'll be all right though, Mum, I knew this was going to happen. I'm ready.'

She gave me another big squeeze and sent me packing. Today wasn't just about saying goodbye to my dog, it was my last full day with my pals. Probably the last time I'd see a couple of them.

I boarded the bus.

'Take your time, loser!' piped up Ellie.

Business as usual then.

The bus seemed a little bit different today, even though the vibe was one I was very used to indeed. It was nervous tension, and it had been with us in buckets back in those early days when we were attempting to size one another up, but now we were nervous for completely different reasons – we weren't sure how to act nice. That's the problem when you've spent most of your life labelled a troubled teen: it's hard to behave in any other way. In my heart I wanted to skip around Canine Partners with a Joker grin on my face, hugging everyone enthusiastically and cooing about how wonderful they had been to me. I wanted to dart into Nina's office with the world's biggest bunch of flowers and explain loudly so everyone could hear that she had totally changed my life and I could never ever thank her enough. I wanted to thank the dogs, individually, even the surly half-poodle that I wasn't entirely sure about. But instead, I was probably going to wander around awkwardly with my hands in my pockets mumbling gratitude like I was being forced to say thank you at knife-point.

'I'm kind of sad,' announced Rob. 'I'm actually going to miss this.'

'Me too!' yapped Katrina, breaking what was normally a pretty long unspoken journey for her.

'Safe to say we're all going to miss this.' Ellie nodded, popping an arm around Allie's shoulder.

I was yet to add my bit, and the options were excruciating. I could join in with the happy sentiment and share another gooey moment like the group hug before the big show, or I could muster up one of my legendary quips about how I wasn't going to miss any of those losers and I'd be glad to be finally rid of them.

'I'm going to miss it too,' I muttered, 'big-time.'

I was going to go for 'like a hole in the head', but at the last second I'd aborted that idea. These people were close friends, I should be comfortable telling them how I felt.

'I'm a tad nervous about saying goodbye to the dogs,' whispered Rob to me, as if it were something to be ashamed and embarrassed about. 'Is that weird?'

'Not at all, man, I'm nervous too. I've tried saying goodbye to Aero a couple of times and it feels wrong.'

'But they're about to go off to new owners . . .'

'I know! It's going to be odd.'

'I might get a little bit jealous. What if he prefers the guy in the wheelchair?'

'It's what we've been training them for, Rob.' I nodded with a certain gravitas, like a Jedi master talking to one of his younglings – as if I knew any of the answers!

We spent the rest of the journey in quiet contemplation, everyone pretending to stare out of the window, but probably deep in thought about how hard today was going to be emotionally. I'd been over it a thousand times in my head, so chose instead to concentrate on the condensation on the minibus window, amusing myself by racing the drops of old rain as they slalomed from top to bottom. Behind them the Chichester town streets became quieter and quieter until they morphed into countryside and the world became an expansive green area. I'd often imagined how it would feel to sprint through all those open fields. I'd love to take Aero with me. We could spend the days hurtling around in the great outdoors, then the evening building campfires and toasting marshmallows and boiling beans. Alternatively, I could just live at Mum and Dad's. Yeah, that would probably be easier.

We pulled into the Canine Partners driveway, which wasn't really a driveway, more a bendy, swirling road that went on for about a mile. There was a similar buzz about the place as we'd experienced on the day of the big show: the dogs were close to graduation, it was the last day of filming, and everyone knew we were there to bid our final farewells.

Nina greeted us all with open arms, dishing out hugs individually. 'Welcome to the last hurrah, kids!' she boomed. 'And I never thought I'd say this, but it's been a bloody pleasure!'

We all laughed. She looked emotional and proud and about a million other great things. She was wearing more lipstick than usual, for some reason. Today was going to be all about having fun, and we had even been promised a decent picnic lunch, which the girls seemed particularly excited about. We were going to get some cool certificates proving that we had been training dogs after all, and we'd been instructed that the guys making the TV show would need to take us each to one side to do short interviews which they could include when the show aired. They'd been doing this sporadically throughout the course, but this was going to be a bigger one to fill any gaps they might have. We'd been told that we might even have to do more than one take, which sounded very professional. Most of us had forgotten about the television programme being made.

'Does my hair look all right?' I asked the camerawoman, who was used to my misplaced vanity.

'It looks fine, Liam.' She sighed.

'But does it look good? If this is going out on telly I need it to look good. Kids at school are going to see this.'

'It looks how it always does, Liam.'

'Is this thing filming?'

I could see the little red light on the camera, which meant it was whirring away, taking actual footage of me, although so far my scenes had mostly hit the cutting-room floor.

'Can you sum up your time at Canine Partners?'

'Good, it's been good.'

A disgruntled face peered at me from behind the camera and the red light disappeared. 'For Christ's sake, Liam, come on, we're going to need more than that.'

'Okay, it's been perfect, it's been emotional, it's made me a better person. I was nothing but a cheeky little bastard when I started on this journey, and now I'm a man and I've learned how to do something useful for once.'

'Right, try again, Liam, but this time, do me a favour, try not to be so bloody sarcastic.'

The ridiculous thing is that I wasn't being sarcastic at all, I completely meant all I'd said. But my voice had an unfortunate timbre, which is so monotone that I do sound sarcastic all the time. As you can imagine, this goes down just brilliantly at school.

After a few takes, we'd covered pretty much everything, and it was a wrap – as they say in show business.

Rob, of course, demanded more camera time than most, delaying the start of our delicious picnic lunch.

'Hurry up, mate!' I shouted over, which apparently caused enough commotion to warrant another take.

The table was awash with brilliant treats. Sandwiches had been sliced into impressive triangles, enough for a royal feast. Plates were piled high with bite-size sausage rolls, mini pizzas, bits of cheese on toothpicks (or cocktail sticks), little sausages, some quiche, bowls of crisps, and, of course, treats for the dogs, who were scheduled to join us for this celebratory luncheon. It was going to be great, the perfect icing on what had been a fantastic cake, but even so I was overcome with that strange, nervous sensation that had infected my bloodstream every time I saw Lian in those first few weeks. It was like I was about to have a date with Aero – a strange thought which I didn't want to dwell on.

It was weird, I had grown so accustomed to my little pal that I was more myself in front of him than I had ever been with any human being. But now I was shy of him again – a bit like I had been on that first meeting all those moons ago. My hands were sweating and my mind was racing. I wasn't sure how to greet him. Would he even know that this great meal we were about to tuck in to was the last supper? That after this there would be no more Liam and Aero, no more pretend washing machines for us to empty, no more seriously misjudged games of Frisbee catch?

I secretly shovelled a handful of cheese into my mouth – something about the process of eating had always calmed me down, I'm not sure why. How I'm not one of those obese teens you see in the tabloid newspapers I have no idea.

'Oi, I saw that!' shouted Ellie. 'We're not supposed to start yet!'

I mumbled an apology through a mouthful of Cheddar from a stick. In the distance Rob was making his way to the picnic area, having finally made it through his last filming session.

'So where are the dogs?' he asked as he rocked up to the table, his eyes darting around the plates of food, as he formulated his plan of where to start first.

'They're being delivered to us.' Ellie beamed.

And with that, the chorus of excited yaps started as our loving hounds rushed over to get stuck into some high-quality nosh. They'd been catered for with extra-special treats for dogs that like to party, and silver bowls overflowing with all sorts of meaty goodness. It was a feast fit for a king, no doubt about it.

I had my back to the dogs and could scarcely bear to look at Aero. I thought I'd start weeping hysterically on the spot, and everyone would laugh at me, so I turned myself around slowly, squinting at the dogs. I didn't want to catch his eye. They were drawing ever closer, I could hear their breathing getting louder and louder, and eventually I felt Aero's nose poke my leg, his paw tapping my foot. I looked down at him; he looked cheerful. I smiled and gave him a good stroke.

This was going to be tough.

'Hello, boy,' I said finally, still a bit shy, but strong enough to put a brave face on it, as if it were just another day for me and my pal. The words came out a little more weak and watery than they usually would, of course, but I don't think anyone noticed.

In fact, everyone was so transfixed by the edible treats on show that I could probably have started screaming hysterically and it would still have taken them a minute or so to peel their eyes away from the great buffet.

It looked ridiculous, the dogs and staff all eating at the same time and place, like some weird school disco night. Most of the dogs were pretty much huddled together, while the rest of us loitered on the other side of the imaginary dance floor, no one sure who should venture across the divide first. Of course, it wasn't really like that at all for the others, just me, mainly because I'd been dreading this day and was feeling more than a little sensitive, thank you very much. The other kids were happily nattering away to each other, allowing their dogs some valuable eating time, but once I'd connected with Aero I couldn't shift away from him. I felt a bit like one of those kids who turn up at primary school on the first day and spend the next hour gripping on to their mum's leg pleading with her not to leave. Aero was my main reason for being here, and I was scared that the minute he left, old Liam would come back, and all the good work that we'd done over the course would somehow be undone. I would turn into that troubled teen with crippling uncontrollable ADHD again. I couldn't bear it.

Aero had helped build new Liam, and I really liked new Liam (even if I do say so myself): he was a thoughtful, confident friend, son, student and boyfriend. My transformation, my new outlook on life were solely down to this amazing dog of mine. Everything was so bright and rosy and brilliant, I was afraid the light switch might be flicked off and everything would go dark again. So, like the toddler holding desperately on to his mother, I knelt beside Aero, persistently stroking him, offering unnecessary words of encouragement, while he wanted to concentrate on eating.

Deep down I knew that this should be a celebration of our time together, and that's why it had been set up – so that we could enjoy a few final moments with our dogs and the Canine

Partners staff – but I was secretly hoping that Nina would notice how close we were and decide that Aero was probably better off staying with me. I could tour the country with him, demonstrating all the strange, brilliant and bizarre feats that Canine Partners dogs are capable of – we'd draw the crowds, yes, sir. We'd definitely draw them in.

Unfortunately, by making such an almighty over-the-top effort to showcase how amazingly we'd bonded, I had accidentally morphed into the world's most annoying and needy teenager. In fact, in many ways, I was behaving rather like a puppy, which would be ironic if it weren't so tragic. Aero just wanted to eat, drink and make merry, but there I was with my over-enthusiastic displays of affection, all sense of shyness totally evaporated in a hysterical display of how best to irritate a dog that you've just trained to undertake such amazing tasks as to empty a washing machine, open doors and call lifts.

'Liam, why don't you leave Aero to eat and come and tuck in?'

'Oh, I'm okay. I'm happy, thanks, Nina, just enjoying a nice lunch with my favourite dog, aren't I, Aero?' I gave him a fervent stroke. 'Aw, look at him, he *loves* me!'

I started giggling like a maniac. What was happening to me?

Eventually enough was enough. Aero yapped at me in what could have been an irritated tone, and the effect was the same as a hypnotist snapping his fingers on stage, bringing back to consciousness one of his unfortunate victims who had spent the last twenty minutes pretending to be a chicken in front of a guffawing audience. I suddenly woke up. What the hell was I doing? I thought. I'm being totally annoying, and there was a table full of meaty treats to demolish. Today was always going to be difficult, but I needed to chill the hell out and enjoy our last few hours together, not turn it into an ordeal. I patted Aero as a way of apologizing for being clingy, and took my seat with the others.

Rob and Ellie were making fast work of the picnic, while Katrina took her time to nibble patiently on a cheese and pickle sandwich. I grabbed a plate, and in one movement swept what seemed like a thousand mini pizzas, two hundred cheesy sticks and some seventy or so sandwiches into a pile, and began attacking them with extremely greedy intentions and gusto. This was the good stuff, all right.

'Right, kids, I think this is a great time to go around the table and say a few words about our experience here. I'll start. It's been a joy, we've had our ups and downs, and there were times when I thought I'd made a massive mistake taking on board a load of crazy young teens, but you've all made me very proud, and I've grown fond of each and every one of you, so well done, and thank you.' Nina welled up as she spoke, her fierce eyes going all dewy.

For the briefest of seconds, I had a chilling flashback to that first day in the hall when we had to go around the room introducing ourselves. I had been petrified and shy, Katrina had been completely unable to speak, and Rob had been totally impossible to shut up. Back then, I had wanted to crawl under a rock, or run away and hide in a cave; the thought of people listening and looking at me had damn near brought me out in hives. But today it was an utterly different kettle of fish. I actually wanted to say a few words, and make sure that these people knew how important this had been to me. First, I had to wait for Katrina to get to the end of her rambling monologue. Seriously.

'. . . so I think I might even go back to school,' she said. 'It's about time I started socializing with other kids again – and anyway, being home schooled is so dull!'

Everyone erupted into applause. Good on her.

'Liam?' said Nina.

I cleared my throat dramatically, for big laughs of course. It didn't really work, and they just sat smiling, looking at me. Leave the gags to Rob, I mentally noted.

'I'm not going to say too much,' I began, 'because there isn't too much to say, beyond thank you to everyone here for making me a better person, and being patient with me. Above all that, I'd like to thank Aero, my dog, for bringing out the best in me and making me realize that I'm not a total failure after all. I never thought I could do anything like this, but, well, here I am. Seriously, this has been the best experience of my life, and I wouldn't change it for anything. Cheers, everyone!'

Everyone clapped and smiled at me.

And then Rob stood up, and we all settled in, ready for hours of material. Out of the corner of my eye I spotted Nina checking her watch. We knew this kid could talk.

'Nice one,' he chirped with two thumbs up, then sat down and continued scoffing his lunch.

Brilliant.

The atmosphere around the table was calm and happy, as we all stuffed our faces and chuckled about the ups and downs we had been through together during the making of this TV show.

'I'm sorry for mocking your moustache that day, Liam,' said Ellie, obviously scanning my top lip to check that I hadn't made the same mistake twice. I hadn't.

'Honestly, Ellie, I think it was for the best. I asked Lian what she thought about guys with moustaches and she's not a fan, so had I had one I might not have a girlfriend now. So, in a way, thank you.'

'Happy to help.'

I apologized mostly for my bad language and the times I'd been surly and aggressive. Everyone appeared to forgive me.

The telly guys had finished packing up their van with equipment – lights, massive furry microphones, heavy-looking film cameras, those clapperboards that signal when they're about to start filming – and came over to say goodbye. I gave them all a mature handshake.

'Right, let's clear up everything, get the dogs sorted, and

pack you little terrors off back to where you belong!' said Nina, clapping her hands together. It was our cue to go, quite obviously.

Thankfully – for clearing-up purposes – most of the food had been consumed, and someone had been clever enough to ship in a load of paper plates, so most of the remains of this luxury wrap party could just go in the bin.

I asked Nina if I could take Aero out in the field one last time, and she told me that of course I could, but I'd have to be quick. It was almost time to bundle us into the bus and be shot of us for good. I put a leash on him and we wandered off to the field, looking something like a toddler having a stroll with their dad.

'So this is it, old pal,' I said, throwing the ball just a few yards away, so as not to have to shout my farewells too loudly. 'It's been a long journey for you and me, but look at us now: you look like a fully grown adult dog, and I'm thinking of actually getting a haircut.'

He dropped the ball enthusiastically at my feet. I picked it up and lobbed it another few yards. Probably about five.

'It's been the best time I've ever had, Aero, and I want you to make sure that you don't stop learning just because I'm not around any more, because there is still a lot you need to do. And remember, your new owner will need you to behave, he won't be as physically capable as me.'

Another throw of the ball, but this one went a little far, so I stood silently as Aero scampered after it, it bounced up, he caught it in his mouth brilliantly, then lurched back to me. Why couldn't he do that with the Frisbee?

'And don't you worry too much about me either, I'm a new guy now, I'll be just fine. I'm doing pretty well at school – Mr Blackmore even thinks I might get a couple of GCSEs, imagine that! I'm not as angry as I was with the world either, little buddy, and Lian really likes me, and I really like her too. It's a shame you two didn't get to hang out more. You'd have liked Mum as well, if you'd got to know her. But I've told her all about you, and I know she thinks that you're brilliant; she always tells me how much I've changed and how nice I've become since I met you.'

I lobbed the tennis ball.

'Don't be scared of going up north either. I've been researching it on the Internet, and it's not as bad as I'd been told. It only rains a little bit, probably not much more than down here, and the parks up there are actually better than some of the ones in the south, and there's a lot of countryside filled with cows and sheep and horses and stuff. People do sound funny though, but I'm sure you'll get used to that, you're a clever dog, aren't you?'

I put the ball in my pocket, sat down on the field and we had a great big slobbery doggy hug.

'I've even had a chat with Nina about the things you like and what you're not so keen on, so she knows what to say to your new owner. I might write it into a list at some point, but she knows the basics. I hope you don't mind, but I told her that you don't enjoy playing Frisbee. I just thought you'd rather your new owner sticks to a tennis ball when you're playing together . . .'

The thought made me suddenly start crying. I didn't want him to play with anyone else.

'Don't forget to do all your chores,' I continued through the tears. 'He won't want to play as often as I like to, so make sure you stay calm when you have to, and don't make him angry; and don't forget me, Aero, please don't forget me. I won't forget you.'

I hugged him and wept; he yapped and licked my face. I walked him back to the kennel, knowing for sure that I'd probably never see him again. We'd never get to play again, we wouldn't learn any new tricks together, I couldn't talk through my problems with him. We were sure going to miss each other, I told myself.

'I love you, you hairy little idiot,' I yelled behind him. He looked around and woofed. He loved me too.

The minibus drove us home in complete silence. We hadn't suddenly run out of things to say, but we just needed to digest everything that had happened at Canine Partners. There were hugs all round as I got off the bus.

'I'll see you soon, guys!'

'Will do, Liam,' they all chirped.

And off I went back to my old life.

12

Another new beginning, and
a bright one too

It did feel strange at first – but, like dogs, human beings are pretty adaptable. So I simply slotted back into my old routine, scraping myself out of bed in the mornings, dragging myself to school, trudging home at the end of the day. There were moments of sunshine and laughter during the days, mainly if I saw my beautiful girlfriend Lian – which I did almost every morning, to be precise – or if I had an art class, where I had developed a fine line in drawing picture-perfect Labrador retrievers. But there was constantly something slightly amiss, a hollowness in the pit of my stomach that just wouldn't go away. It didn't take a scientist or a doctor to figure out what it might be. I was missing Aero, I was missing Canine Partners, I was missing that whole period of my life.

I've heard people say that it's easy to look back on things through rose-tinted glasses, but that wasn't the case at all here. Sometimes I would even try to focus on the bad times, the tellings-off from Nina, the times when the others would pick on me about my facial hair experiments. But nothing could shift the sense that I had found the place where I belonged, but I wasn't there any more. I felt like a soldier without a gun, a trucker without a truck, a caretaker without a broom – you get the picture. The point being that this was all wrong. I was a dog trainer, damn it! It was in my blood.

'You've got to finish school first, darling,' said Mum. 'Then you can think about what you want to do next, but focus on your exams for now, they're important.'

I had, of course, been overcome by an urge to take life by the scruff of the neck, pack up all my belongings into a giant rucksack and head off into the sunset to train dogs to help disabled people until my dying day. Mum, however, had hit me with some logic. She was right, school was the first priority. New mature Liam knew that – Aero knew that too. School was important, and I'd need to get a few GCSEs just to survive in the real world.

Even so, not a day went by when I didn't spare a thought for my furry pal, shivering up there in the north, zipping around the icy parks not catching Frisbees. I knew he'd be spreading a bit of sunshine wherever he went, though.

The weeks turned into months. Of our motley group, I'd still see Rob from time to time; our friendship had stayed strong, and since the course he'd somehow managed to get a place at a performing arts school, and hadn't yet been booted out! His tantrums had become a rarity, as had my visits to detention. I'd love to say that they were completely non-existent, but I'm not a totally spot-changing leopard, and remnants of the old me were still lurking under the surface. But for the most part, things were great.

'It's starting!' yelled Mum from the bottom of the stairs, and down I stumbled. The lounge was packed with friends and relatives for my television debut. *The Doghouse* was the chosen title, and that was me all right, up there on the telly – all long hair, massive trousers and surly looks. It was so surreal watching myself, seeing my mannerisms that I was quite unaware of, and hearing my voice, which had never sounded so expressionless and monotonous. The first episode made for pretty hard viewing – we were a truly terrible bunch.

Mum looked over at me. 'See what you were like?' she said, half laughing, half totally serious.

'Mum, I am so sorry,' I replied, and I meant it. To watch myself moping around grumbling about things was really embarrassing. I could only bear it because I knew all about the happy ending to this story, and I knew for a fact that they had captured some brilliant footage of me and Aero doing amazing feats of amazingness. They were bound to use all of it! (Sadly, they didn't.)

As expected, being on television had made me a minor celebrity around school – for a few short weeks anyway. I'd gone into this whole experiment in the first place for the bragging rights, but now that people had seen me on the small screen it didn't seem to matter. The whole television side of the course had vanished into the background the minute I'd started bonding with Aero. So when people began to chuckle and go on at me for being on telly, it didn't feel as excellent as I'd hoped it would. Although, I'm not going to lie, I did enjoy the attention I got from girls, mainly because it worked wonders for my relationship with Lian. It's like Ellie had told me all those months ago, nothing makes you more desirable than a little bit of interest from other people.

'Hey, gorgeous, aren't you that boy off the dog programme?' yelled a girl's voice from the other side of the street, and without even turning around to see who it was, Lian just hollered, 'Back off,' over her shoulder. It was great, after months of wooing and dating, and treating my girl to presents and meals and cinema trips to make her like me, she was the one doing all the work to keep me on a tight leash.

Ellie and the girls would be very impressed, I'm sure.

'I love you, Liam, you know that, right?' she whispered into my ear as we sat in the park watching the sun go down one Saturday evening.

'I know,' I croaked in the least cool voice possible, 'and, um, I . . . er . . . love, um, you know, like, you . . . innit.'

It was the most romantic moment ever.

Of course, it wasn't long before everyone had forgotten all about my brief television career, and I was back to being just another average Joe.

But while the moments with the spotlight shining directly

into my eyes had faded, my absolute obsession with everything I'd learned during that time just wouldn't go away no
matter what I did. The idea at the outset had been to train the
dogs, train ourselves, and go away into the real world as better
people – that was the brief, and all that had happened to me
and then some. And yet, I still felt that something was missing;
the empty feeling wasn't going anywhere in a hurry. I'd had a
lifetime of feeling like the odd one out, but I had finally found
somewhere I belonged and could stay calm, happy and out of
trouble.

After days of constant pestering and a little bit of dramatic
moping, I finally persuaded Mum to take some time out and
give me a lift to my old haunt. It was strange heading out there
into the countryside without the rattle of an old minibus and
my four tearaway companions nattering away alongside me.
Instead we glided through the country roads in silence, looking out across the fields that had seemed so full of space and
freedom, and along the narrow driveway that led all the way up
to Canine Partners. I was going home, and the entire journey,
though it had been months since my last visit, was etched on
my mind, so I knew every millimetre we passed – not a single
view wasn't already accounted for.

I'd dreamed about going back a million times, and so far it
was exactly as I'd envisaged. I felt nervous, since this was the
first time I'd set foot on Canine Partners land as an individual,
not part of a group or a TV show. But above and beyond anything else, I felt excited.

Would they be remotely interested in me now that I was just
a normal teen with no massive behavioural issues to speak of?
Should I even be there without a film crew? In many ways I
felt naked, but thankfully one of those ways wasn't 'literally'.
I had dressed that day.

A strange yet almost entirely predictable thing happened as we
got out of the car: the hole in my tummy disappeared, and the
clouds above my head lifted. It was a moment of absolute belong-

ing. This was exactly where I was supposed to be. I breathed in that great country air, felt it fill my lungs, and exhaled all the inner tension that had niggled me since the show had ended. There was scaffolding and building work taking place in the courtyard, so business was obviously booming, and the centre was expanding. No wonder, these dogs were the best. I knew that.

It was like striding around an old primary school – everything seemed so much smaller and quainter than I remembered. I had found it completely impossible to imagine life at Canine Partners going on without me, but judging by all the activity around me, it had gone from strength to strength. I walked into the lobby, I looked in on the dogs in the hall being trained to open doors by some trainers I had never seen before. They were doing a great job.

'Ah, Mr Creed!' boomed a loud womanly voice behind me. It was Nina, looking exactly as radiant and fantastic as I remembered. She gave me a great big bear hug; it was excellent to see her too.

'The place looks amazing,' I gushed. 'What's with all the building work?'

'Oh, we're expanding, Liam, training more dogs, really getting this show on the road – the demand for them is sky-rocketing.'

I definitely wanted to be part of this. Nina explained every-thing that was going on: they were building digs for the trainers, more than double the number of dogs were being trained this year, and everything was super-duper. And yet, all the while, I wanted to say just one thing. I had to stop myself from blurting it out.

'Erm, I, um . . . I was thinking, well, wondering if I . . . ah . . . could . . .'

'I see you've overcome your shyness!' Nina chuckled.

I took a deep breath. 'I want to come back, Nina. Can I?'

At this point, I was hoping that Nina would punch the sky and insist that I leave school and start at Canine Partners immediately – thank heavens I'd realized my calling. But as with most things in my life, it wasn't quite that simple.

'Liam, I would love to have you back, but it wouldn't be the same as before, you wouldn't just walk in and become a trainer – that was a project for a TV show.'

'Then what could I do, Nina? I'm completely serious about this.'

'Do as we all do, then. Start at the bottom and you build your way up from there. We don't have a job for you, but I'm more than happy for you to volunteer and help out.'

It was a no-brainer. I just wanted to be there again and this was my route back in. Of course, I'd have loved to have been fast-tracked to the top, but if getting there was going to mean weeks of clearing up dog poo, and filling up water bowls, then so be it. I was embarking on a lifetime's work, and baby steps were just fine with me. Plus, being a schoolboy, it was going to have to be one day a week.

And, yes, Nina wasn't lying – the volunteering job was nothing like the old one. It had been so easy for me back then. Aero was practically delivered to me on a shiny platter, and I hadn't paid much attention to what might be going on behind the scenes, but now I was one of the troopers in the trenches doing the jobs that only really dedicated dog lovers would do. Essentially that means that I was dealing with the smellier areas of dog ownership. Clearing up behind them, making sure the kennels were in good nick, scrubbing and cleaning yapping pups. I was at the bottom of a very long ladder. I was doing this all for love, no money was changing hands, and I was happier than a pig in muck.

Everyone around me told me they had noticed how my bounce had returned.

During those first few weeks skipping around Canine Partners, I was confined to two areas – the kennels and the washroom. Those places were my work station, and I'd spend the day swinging between them in a haze of yapping, barking and panting. Not to mention all the noises the dogs made! Then, one day, I was called into the offices to collect some important training instructions and posters to put up around the building.

I bounced into the plush office building looking like something a Labrador might traipse in on his paw, hopped into the lift to save time, and went up all of one floor.

'Ah yes, hi, Liam, here are those posters for you,' said Nina, handing them over. 'Make sure you stick them all up, won't you?'

'Aye-aye, skip!' I cheered, doing a salute, and off I went. Through the double doors, down the small corridor, and past the loos – until I stopped in my tracks, completely frozen.

There it was, some ten feet away from me, looking down over me, as the rest of the world melted into a muffle, and time stopped for all of about ten seconds. I walked slowly towards it, feeling every single beat of my heart as if it were about to explode through my chest. I was completely stumped, and thank goodness there was no one around to witness my terrible unprofessionalism, as a handful of posters and training information dropped to my feet in a big papery bundle. I stared for a minute, then I felt a gigantic swell of pride, mixed with sadness, sweep over me. How this was a surprise, I don't know, but for some reason, it just was.

I'd seen the Hall of Fame a million times before, but back then it had just been a load of pictures of dogs that I didn't know sitting proudly with their owners.

But this wasn't just any old dog, this was my best friend, the dog that I trained.

The dog that trained me.

'Aero' it read on the plaque beneath the framed photograph. He'd grown, and looked as scruffy and cheerful as usual; next to him was his proud owner, beaming from a wheelchair – he had kind laughing eyes, and the pair looked close. They were happy together, and a tidal wave of joy surged through me, and the world's biggest grin spread across my face.

'Good on you, mate,' I said to the picture. 'I'm so proud of you.'

I gathered together all the stray pages littering the floor, winked at the picture and bounded downstairs to do as instructed.

I've said it before, and I'll say it again: I owe everything to that dog.

Acknowledgements

I would like to thank the following people: Mum and Dad for always being there for me no matter what, Aero for helping me realise my worth, Canine Partners for putting up with me, Nina, Mr Blackmore because without him none of this would have happened, Jason Cummings, Rob, Jaimie the cameraman, Lorraine my other youth worker and my brother Mathew and sister Sophie, who have always stood by me.